D0783788

Non fiction Gift Aid
£

0 031140 014138

20/23   £3

FLAVOURED SPIRITS

1,000 BC onwards (all flavours)

FLAVOURED INFUSIONS, SPIRITS AND THE LAW

In the UK people are free to make *naturally fermented* alcohol for their own use, and the development of special alcohol-tolerant yeasts has made the production of liqueur and spirit-based drinks from high alcohol washes (typically 20% ABV) a practical proposition. However, *it is illegal to manufacture spirits* without a distiller's licence, which is required under the provisions of Section 12 of the Alcoholic Liquor Duties Act 1979. This includes the manufacture of spirits for your own or domestic use. Contact HMRC's advice service on 0845 010 9000 or visit their website to read Public Notice 39 (https://www.gov.uk/government/publications/excise-notice-39-spirits-production-in-the-uk).

Unless credited, photographs are supplied by Shutterstock and istock. Additional images supplied by Cath Harries.

© Tim Hampson 2017

All rights reserved. No part of this publication may be reproduced or stored in a retrieval system or transmitted, in any form or by any means, electronic, mechanical, photocopying, recording or otherwise, without prior permission in writing from Haynes Publishing.

Tim Hampson has asserted his moral rights to be identified as the author of this work.

First published in May 2017

A catalogue record for this book is available from the British Library

ISBN 978 1 78521 087 7

Library of Congress control no. 2016959359

Published by Haynes Publishing,
Sparkford, Yeovil,
Somerset BA22 7JJ, UK.
Tel: 01963 440635
Int. tel: +44 1963 440635
Website: www.haynes.com

Haynes North America Inc.,
85 Lawrence Drive, Newbury Park,
California 91320, USA.

Printed in Malaysia.

FLAVOURED SPIRITS

1,000 BC onwards (all flavours)

Enthusiasts' Manual

A practical guide to the history, appreciation and making of flavoured spirit infusions

Tim Hampson

CONTENTS

INTRODUCTION

First take a spirit, be it vodka, gin, whisky or even brandy – indeed, it could be any distilled spirit; then add some fruit or other flavouring, and you have an infusion. Sweeten this with sugar and you have a liqueur, a word derived from Latin *liquifacere*, meaning to dissolve or melt. According to the *Oxford English Dictionary* a liqueur is a strong alcoholic liquor which has been sweetened and flavoured with an aromatic substance. It is first found in the English language in 1255.

The origins of liqueurs are probably medicinal, but they could be mystical. In the Middle Ages (11–15th centuries) monastic orders were the centres of temporal learning and physical healing in Europe. Most monasteries had their own sweet-smelling herb garden, in which they grew the ingredients they needed for their potions and remedies, which were usually prepared in the form of infusions. (One of these early liqueurs is Chartreuse, made by monks from an ancient recipe.)

Over time it was discovered that the healing qualities of herbs and spices seemed to be enhanced and enriched if they were steeped in alcohol. However, like many medicines most remained barely palatable until the monks discovered that if they added honey or sugar to the mix its flavour improved – the origin of our phrase 'to sugar the pill'. It's possible that Crusaders returning from the East in the 11th–14th centuries brought refined sugar with them, though by the end of the 16th century it was being widely grown not just in the East but in the West Indies.

Today many of the finest commercial liqueurs maintain their monastic origins and are still produced by religious orders, or in seaports where sugar and other exotic ingredients were originally imported into Europe. Over time monastic tinctures evolved from palatable medicines into pleasing drinks.

And then the world discovered cocktails – mixed drinks that can be imbibed either neat or as part of a larger drink. Many cocktails are based on a neutral spirit, but any spirit can be used to make such infusions. The intensely orange-flavoured Grand Marnier has a cognac base, while Drambuie is made from whisky, heather, honey and herbs. Indeed, all the best liqueurs are made by infusing the flavouring ingredients – be they fruit, herbs, beans, nuts, spices or even meat – in a spirit and then adding sugar. Some are drinkable immediately, while others require a little time to draw the flavour from their ingredients.

The distinction between a flavoured spirit and a liqueur can seem vague, since the terms are often interchanged. Many of the diverse ingredients required for making both will already be present in most kitchens, and the others are easily sourced, which means that with very little equipment and only a small amount of work exotic-tasting liqueurs can be made at home. Consequently it's pretty easy and a lot of fun to create your own drinks. Put them into a nice bottle or container and you have the perfect gift to share with friends.

◀ **A stained glass window at the Benedictine distillery shows the monks at work.** (Courtesy Benedictine)

▶ **The huge barrels in the cellar of the Benedictine Abbey of Monte Oliveto Maggiore, Tuscany, Italy.**

A concentrated history of distillation

The mystic alchemist raised his eyes to the sky, and with a practised motion poured a small amount of a clear liquid on to a flame. With a flash it burst into a large conflagration. The spirit of life was born! Well, the description is fanciful, but it's easy to imagine early people being amazed by the process and seeing spiritual significance in the shaman's trick.

But when did we start to distil, and why? We don't know for sure, but the term 'spirit' was first used in reference to distillations concocted by pioneer Middle Eastern physicians and alchemists intent on producing medicinal elixirs, balms and perfumes rather than inventing flavoursome alcoholic drinks.

There's some evidence that suggests the Babylonians of Mesopotamia were practising simple distilling as early as the second millennium BC, while some historians believe that distilling began in China a thousand years earlier. Certainly by 200 BC the Romans were boiling and bubbling ingredients to make concentrations of liquids. Archaeological evidence indicates that many of the earliest distillers probably worked with rose petals and lavender water, which were both highly regarded for their medicinal and culinary qualities.

The equipment used was pretty basic and probably not that effective or efficient. Steam probably rose from a boiling pot of petals and leaves and was collected in concentrated form in a lid of some sort. By the time we get to the first century AD there's definite evidence from Egypt of distillers

▲ The Greek god of wine, Dionysius, is still associated with wine, intoxication and partying to excess.

◀ The Greeks and Romans brewed and distilled extensively, and exported wine all over the known world. These amphorae, used to transport wine, were found in modern day Turkey.

▲ A woodcut from the Middle Ages showing an alchemist's laboratory. Distillation was an important alchemical art.

▼ The early alchemists used a variety of herbs and spices to produce elixirs, balms and perfumes.

being hard at work. Again, it wasn't a drink that was being made but *sulphur water* or *divine water*, generated during experiments at turning base metals into gold. Others believe the early distillers were creating 'liquid fire' – some kind of concentrate that was highly flammable. To wise men of the time, fire was the highest and most important element, and if at some point such early distillers tried to distil liquids made from grapes or even cereals it was not to produce a proto-brandy or whisky, but rather for the fire content created during their experiments.

When Dionysus, the son of the Greek god Zeus, was honoured with elaborate ceremonies at Delphi and other Northern Greek cities from the fifth century BC onwards, wine was distilled and the flaming of the resultant liquid was part of the ritual used to honour this god of wine. Similarly Demeter, the Greek earth goddess responsible for fertile well-ordered societies, was honoured with rituals using grain that was very probably distilled.

It was this period that gave us the 'alembic pot still' or 'alchemical still' used for distilling chemicals, consisting of two vessels connected by a tube. The liquid to be distilled is boiled in the first, slightly larger container, with the vapour rising into the alembic hood, where it cools, condenses and runs down the spout into the other container. A modern-day spirit distiller would recognise this equipment as a 'pot still'.

▲ The spirit from medieval alembic stills, very like this one, was used as a medicine to cure all manner of ills.

▲ Monasteries became important places for the making of potions and medicines, and later liqueurs. (Courtesy Benedictine)

Moving on a thousand years or so, to Bologna in what is now Northern Italy, word began to spread about a distilled liquid with almost magical qualities described as *aqua vitae* – the water of life. Indeed, it was a liquid with seemingly miraculous qualities; said to cure colds, pains in the head, trembling, toothaches and even bad breath. *Eau-de-vie* or water of life was likewise the name given by Arnau de Vilanova – according to some historians the first man to distil wines in France in the 13th century – to

▼ The impressive, highly decorated, 19th century-built Benedictine Palace, in Fécamp, where the famous liqueur is distilled today. (Courtesy Benedictine)

the by-product that resulted from his distillation process. He attributed to it the virtue of prolonging life.

Knowledge of aqua vitae spread quickly, though Church authorities weren't yet ready to accept medicines which had been created by alchemy, since they believed illness was cured by God's will and not human intervention. Eventually, however, the Church overcame its opposition to distilled medicines so that by the early 14th century many monasteries had stills for making aqua vitae. No doubt much experimentation must have gone on as the monks created medicines and healing liquids using herbs from their gardens – the precursors, no doubt, of modern liqueurs such as Benedictine and Chartreuse.

By 1378 distillers in Italy were supplying distilled liquid to the public, and the largest households even had their own stills. The authorities consequently started to become concerned about the consumption of spirits, as people without specialist knowledge set up their own stills and sold flavoured spirits.

The monasteries became an important influence in the spread of knowledge about distillation, and at some point ale rather than wine began to be distilled in the search for new and better infusions. Irish whiskey and German brandy were already available in the 12th century and by the 1500s consumption of such drinks had become widespread. Thus began the national drinks of Europe – gin in England, jenever in the Netherlands and Belgium, schnapps in Germany, akavit in Scandinavia, vodka in Russia and other parts of Eastern Europe, poitin in Ireland, rakia in the Balkans and ouzo in Greece.

The earliest documented record of distilling in Scotland dates to 1494, when an entry in the Exchequer Rolls listed 'Eight bolls of malt to Friar John Cor wherewith to make aqua vitae'. Clearly distillation was now a well-established practice. *Uisquebaugh*, the Gaelic translation of aqua vitae, was known for its medicinal qualities, being prescribed for the preservation of health, the prolongation of life and the relief of colic, palsy, smallpox and a host of other ailments. It was given to babies, children and adults alike.

Today a little of what you fancy will definitely do you good, and a homemade infusion will probably taste much better than the ancient medicines – though it probably won't cure palsy or smallpox!

▲ By the 14th century stills were becoming commonplace across Europe to produce flavoured spirits.

▼ By the 19th century distillation was no longer confined to religious orders or large households and had become commonplace. In rural France, many people distilled wine using fruit from their own harvests.

HERBS AND SPICES

Timeline

Herbs and spices played an essential part in the shaping of world history and have been a huge source of wealth and revenue. They have been responsible for the opening up of major trade routes, advances in medical science and the development of many drinks.

Prehistory

Archaeological information suggests that hunters and gatherers from the very earliest days of human history, wrapped meat in leaves, and many plants are thought to have been used for medicinal reasons. If the leaves, seeds or roots they used had a pleasant taste or odour it's thought likely they would have been subsequently used as condiments.

▼ The Hebrews, Greeks, and Romans all used cassia bark as a perfume and to cure indigestion.

◢ Fennel was used as an antidote for poisonous herbs, mushrooms and snake bites.

c2700 BC

According to ancient Chinese myths, at about this date the emperor Shen Nung probably wrote *Pen Ts'ao Ching* ('The Classic Herbal'). This early publication mentions more than a hundred medicinal plants including the spice cassia, which is similar to cinnamon.

c1550 BC

One of the earliest documents showing the use of cultivated herbs and spices for medicinal uses, the Ebers papyrus, records their common application in Egypt, and extols their medical benefits. Coriander, fennel, juniper, cumin, garlic and thyme were all thought of as having health-giving properties.

▲ Aromatic coriander seeds were often used to treat people with serious chest infections.

▲ In Roman times, rose petal oil was used for medicinal purposes and perfumes for wealthy citizens.

Records from that time show that the people who built the Great Pyramid of Cheops consumed onion and garlic as a means of promoting health and increasing strength.

c710 BC

There is a clay tablet in the British Museum that lists the plants grown by Merodach-Baladan, king of Babylonia in his garden. The list includes 64 species of plants, and it seems he kept records on how to cultivate many spices and herbs, including cardamom, coriander, garlic, thyme, saffron and turmeric. Sin, the ancient Babylonian god of the moon, was thought to control medicinal plants.

668–627 BC

A scroll of cuneiform writing dating to the reign of King Ashurbanipal of Assyria includes a list of aromatic plants such as thyme, sesame, cardamom, turmeric, saffron, poppy, garlic, cumin, anise, coriander, dill, and myrrh. The Assyrians also used sesame as a cooking oil.

▼ There is a long tradition in Chinese medicine of using star anise to cure colic and indigestion.

559–529 BC

Onions, garlic and shallots became popular ingredients in Persia by the 6th century BC – a surviving record from King Cyrus' time, for instance, details a purchase of 395,000 bunches of garlic. The Persians also distilled essential oils from roses, lilies, coriander and saffron.

c460 BC

Hippocrates, the father of modern medicine, devised a scientific system of treatments that demonstrated the value of herbs in easing pain and curing disease. Early medical texts ascribed to him say much about spices and herbs, including saffron, cinnamon, thyme, coriander, mint and marjoram. Of the more than 400 herbal remedies these books record, at least half remain in use today.

c400 BC

Literature ascribed to the Indian physician and surgeon Susruta reports that white mustard and other aromatic plants

▼ The leaves and petals of various aromatic plants were sought after for their medicinal qualities.

▲ The oil from black and white sesame seeds was thought to have magical qualities – hence the expression 'open sesame'.

▲ Healing flowers and herbs, in particular chamomile, were gathered for distillation into essential oils.

were used on bed sheets to ward off evil. He is also said to have applied a poultice made from sesame paste to post-operative wounds, which may have acted as an antiseptic. By this time a profitable and lucrative herb and spice trade was developing between India and the Near East.

1st century AD

The Greek physician Dioscorides listed the medicinal properties of over 500 plants in his huge work, the *De Materia Medic*. The Romans used herbs and spices brought by sea from India for perfume, cosmetics, medicine, cooking and the flavouring of drinks. Spices were also considered to have properties conducive to good health and were used in poultices and healing plasters. At about the same date the overland route from China, the Silk Road, came into being.

7th century

By this time much of the Middle East, North Africa and parts of southern Europe were dominated by the Islamic Empire. The Islamic caliphates had outstanding scientists who, among other things, developed the process of extracting flower scents from blossoms and herbs and created distillation techniques to create essential oils from aromatic plants.

8th century

An important person in the development and cultivation of various herbs in Northern Europe was Charlemagne, King of the Franks and Emperor of the West, who is believed to have encouraged the cultivation of anise, fennel, fenugreek, sage, thyme, parsley and coriander.

9th century

Arab physicians used a growing number of spices and herbs to formulate syrups and flavouring extracts, and continued to develop distilling techniques.

12th century

During the Middle Ages the flow of goods from East to West dwindled until new trade routes were opened up during the Crusades, after which the herb and spice trade flourished once more. The Italian mercantile cities of Venice and Genoa grew rich as they capitalised on this new trade.

1180

King Henry II founded a pepperer's guild of wholesale merchants in England. Many early spicers and pepperers subsequently became apothecaries and, later, medical practitioners. Some common medical practices included prescribing saffron, garlic soup and juniper wine for health benefits.

1270

Marco Polo set out from Venice to find a new route to the Far East that would bypass the Arab traders, who still controlled the trade and kept prices high. He returned 25 years later, bringing with him new and exotic herbs and spices from China.

14th century

Asian spices in Europe were costly and mainly used by the wealthy. A kilo of saffron cost the same as a horse; a kilo of ginger cost as much as a sheep. A German pricelist of 1393 lists 500g of nutmeg as worth seven fat oxen.

1470–1500

Herbals were among the first books to be printed in both China and, much later in Europe. In 1492 Christopher Columbus set sail from Spain in search of a new route to the Indies. He returned with allspice and chilli peppers from the West Indies. In 1497 The Portuguese explorer Vasco de Gama set out to discover a sea route to the East. He reached Malabar on the west coast of India and returned to Portugal with a cargo of herbs, spices and jewels.

▲ Saffron, a spice derived from the dried stigmas of the crocus flower, is one the most expensive spices in the world.

1519

During his reconnaissance of south-eastern Mexico, the Spanish conquistador Hernán Cortés found vanilla, a spice used by the Aztecs as a flavouring to season their chocolate beverages.

1521

Magellan's fleet completed the first circumnavigation of the earth and returned to Europe with a rich cargo from the Spice Islands (the Moluccas). This age of exploration led to an increase in the number and variety of imported herbs and spices available in the West.

1545

The first herbal or physic garden, intended to provide plants purely for the purpose of medical studies, was established at the University of Padua in Italy. By this time more and more drinks were being flavoured with spices.

▼ The wealth of many European countries was related to their ability to exploit and control the trade of herbs and spices.

▲ The history of the spice trade is, above all, the history of pepper, king of spices. At one time a single peppercorn was as valuable as a pearl.

1602

The Dutch founded the Dutch East India Company to trade directly with the East for spices. This gave them a monopoly of the spice trade that lasted for nearly 200 years. The Netherlands became known for adding spices to spirits.

End of the 18th century

The British ousted the Dutch from India, and London became the centre of the world's spice trade.

▼ Illustrated herbals, books identifying plants and their uses, became common in Western Europe during the 14th and 15th centuries, but were in existence in ancient Egyptian times.

CHAPTER 2

DISTILLATION

Fermentation

The soul and character of a liqueur comes from whatever spices, fruits, herbs or other ingredients have been used to flavour it. However, its beating heart is the distilled alcohol that gives the drink its kick.

All spirits go through at least two procedures: fermentation and distillation. Fermentation is where the alcohol is created; distillation is where the alcohol is separated, concentrated and removed.

For fermentation to occur, two things are needed: yeast and a raw material in liquid form that contains sugar. Yeast needs sugar as part of its lifecycle. It happily munches, chomps and thrives on it. This way even one yeast cell quickly becomes millions. As part of its energetic and mysterious lifestyle, yeast cells produce carbon dioxide and a waste product that we rather enjoy – alcohol. Putting it simply, fermentation is yeast + sugar = CO2 + alcohol.

Beer is made by fermenting the sugars in barley and other cereals. Wine is made from fermented fruit. Depending on the yeast used, the alcohol in most beers is around 5% ABV (alcohol by volume) and in wines about 14% ABV. It is distillation that takes this alcohol from a relatively low strength

to as high as 80% ABV. Essentially distillation is therefore the concentration of the alcohol in a beer or wine to make it much stronger, a process that's achieved in a still.

SPIRITS

Distilled spirits are produced from natural raw materials such as grapes, other fruit, sugar cane, molasses, potatoes and cereals, and are the first building block in any infusion or liqueur. There are plenty to choose from.

Any fermented plant, fruit, grain or vegetable can be used as the base material for a spirit. If sugar is naturally present in the raw material, as in fruit or molasses, the fermentation can start directly. With grain, however, the initial fermentation will only occur after the naturally occurring starch has been converted into sugar.

In the case of a pot still whisky, barley grain is malted to release the sugar. This means the grain is allowed to start germinating, converting the starch into sugar. The grain is then dried, which stops the germination process. The malted barley

▼ To make brandy, first grapes must be fermented. To stop wine becoming infected modern wineries are almost clinically clean.

is then ready for mashing, the next stage in the process of releasing fermentable sugars.

Some spirits can only be made from specific raw material. Brandy, for instance, is made from grapes. Vodka, on the other hand, can be made from a range of raw materials. Grain is used to produce spirits in Western Europe and sugar cane is used in the West Indies, while in Eastern Europe potatoes are traditionally used.

Some spirits – gin, for instance – are flavoured, while others are both flavoured and sweetened.

▼ Spirits and liqueurs come in many colours and can be packaged in bottles of many shapes and sizes.

▲ The island of Islay in Scotland is home to many beautiful and hard working whisky stills. (Cath Harries)

▼ To make brandy distilled wine will be put into large oak barrels and left to mature for many years.

◄ To release the flavours and aromas from botanicals used to make Benedictine, the ingredients are steeped in hot water, a process similar to making a giant pot of tea. (Courtesy Benedictine)

The distilling process

Many subtleties are involved in the creation of different spirits. By way of example, the process for cereal-based spirits is as follows.

MILLING

The raw material, in this case cereals, is ground into a coarse meal. This breaks down the protective hull covering the raw material and frees the starch that contains the sugars needed for yeast to thrive.

MASHING

The starch is converted to sugar, which is mixed with warm water and then steeped. The process is very similar to making a cup of tea: the goodness is drawn out of the ground grain into the warm water. Brewers and whisky distillers usually call this process 'mashing'.

FERMENTATION

The sweet liquid, which is called 'wort' in a brewery, then has yeast added to it. A source of sugar is vital to the production and lifecycle of yeast cells – indeed, they thrive on it. As the yeast multiplies it produces carbon dioxide, which bubbles away and becomes a mixture of alcohol, grain particles and congeners, or the elements that create the flavour of each drink.

DISTILLATION

The mixture of alcohol, particles and congeners is known as the 'wash' in a whisky distillery but in a brewery would be called beer. This wash is heated in a still, and as the temperature rises the alcohol starts to boil. Drinkable alcohol boils at a lower temperature than water (78.5°C compared to 100°C) and then vaporises, leaving the water, grain particles and congeners behind.

◄ Hubble, bubble, toil and trouble..., a working distillery is a place of heat and swirling steam, needing constant attention from the skilled distillers. (Courtesy Benedictine)

Major spirit styles

- **Applejack** – An American apple brandy.
- **Arak** – A spirit from India, the Middle East, North Africa and the Caribbean. It is made from a variety of raw materials including sugar cane, dates and figs.
- **Armagnac** – A brandy made in the department of Gers in south-eastern France.
- **Brandy** – From probably the 12th century onwards Italian monks and Moorish scholars developed the art of distilling grape wine and making brandy. Before being stored in a wooden barrel the spirit is clear – it is the wooden barrel that gives it colour and taste.
- **Calvados** – A French apple brandy that's stored in oak barrels for two years, is called applejack in North America.
- **Cognac** – A brandy made in the departments of Charente and Charente-Maritime, just north of Bordeaux.
- **Eau de vie** – A distillation of fermented fruits that are matured in glass containers. Made widely in Europe, variants include slivovitz, wasser and geist. Fruit, including pears, cherries and plums, can be added to give it colour and flavour.
- **Gin** – An early medicinal spirit, gin is distilled with a range of botanicals that include juniper, which give it its distinct taste and aroma.
- **Grappa** – Also called *marc* in France, grappa is an Italian brandy produced from the distilled residue left in a barrel after the wine has been decanted.
- **Korn** – A German variant of vodka/schnapps that's usually made from grain, though potatoes can be used. Korn and schnapps are often interchangeable terms.
- **Pisco** – A South American brandy.
- **Rum** – A spirit made from fermented sugar cane. Traditionally made in the Caribbean, it was known as 'kill-devil' and was given to slaves as a cure-all and for payment of work. It is produced in clear and dark forms.
- **Schnapps/akvavit** – Akvavit is a Scandinavian variant of flavoured vodka. It's often flavoured with caraway seeds. The word *schnapps* comes from the Old Norse word *snappen*, meaning to gulp. Traditionally it's drunk ice-cold from small shot glasses.
- **Tequila** – The distillate of blue agave, a spiky lily-like plant that grows in Mexico.
- **Vodka** – The base alcohol for hundreds of cocktails. It can be made from more or less any fermented alcohol, though its name is the Russian word for grain spirits. Easy to make, the clear spirit is diluted and possibly some glycerine is added. It needs no ageing.
- **Whisky** – A spirit usually made from fermented grain. It's aged in wood for at least three years for Scotch whisky and Irish whiskey but two years for an American whiskey. The wooden barrel gives it its colour and flavour. In India some whiskies are made from molasses. Variants include bourbon, Tennessee, Kentucky, Canadian and Japanese.

Types of still

There are two basic kinds of still: the pot and the continuous. A pot still looks like a large kettle and is traditionally fired by direct heat. The vapours collect in the head and feed into a narrow tube from where they go into a condenser, where they are cooled and return to liquid form.

Continuous stills are usually arranged as a series of two vertical columns, called the analyser and rectifier. Steam enters the bottom of the analyser and rises and meets the wash – which has been heated by the rectifier – coming down the column. The alcohol in the wash is vaporised and falls to the bottom of the rectifier. As the hot vapour rises it is cooled by the pipe carrying the cold wash and will condense. This method produces an alcohol with a high degree of purity, but, some might argue, less taste.

The vaporised, steaming alcohol rises up out of the still and is collected. It is then cooled, or condensed, to form clear drops of distilled spirit. In some cases it might be distilled again, and sometimes a third time. The result of this process is a clear, strong and not very palatable raw spirit. All spirit, when it comes off a still, is colourless – any colour in the final drink comes from the ageing process or added colouring.

This raw spirit is sometimes known as moonshine, but if you put it into a wooden barrel and wait three years you'll have whisky. Add glycerine to the spirit and you get vodka. If you add juniper and other botanicals to it you would have gin. In the case of wine, distil it and you have brandy. Rum is made from sugar cane. There are endless variations on the theme, and there are many fruits, vegetables and tubers from which a base alcohol can be made. In many parts of the world potatoes are fermented to make the base alcohol from which vodka is produced.

For the makers of liqueurs it is the base spirit that's the canvas on which they create their drinks. As a very general rule, a neutral base spirit such as an eau de vie will be used to make the liqueurs used for a cocktail. Liqueurs that are often drunk neat are based on specific spirits – sloe gin is gin-based, Grand Marnier has a brandy base and Drambuie a whisky base.

According to many experts the best liqueurs are made by infusing the flavouring ingredient in the spirit and then adding sugar afterwards, rather than at the same time.

▼ Once all stills were heated using direct heat. Such stills can be found in Indonesia, used to make arak from distilled palm juice.

Making liqueurs

There are three main methods of making liqueurs: distillation – used to extract flavours from seeds and flowers; percolation – used to obtain flavours from leaves and herbs; and infusion or maceration – used to extract flavours from fruits, seeds and flowers.

DISTILLING

This is one of the oldest and most important methods of extracting flavours. Herbs, peels and other ingredients are soaked in a distillation that still contains water and alcohol. This mixture is then heated until the liquid evaporates and condenses in the higher reaches of the still.

During evaporation the alcohol draws the essential oils from the herbs, creating a flavourful yet colourless extract called a distillate, which faithfully conveys the flavours of the original ingredients.

PERCOLATION

This is the same process as that by which good coffee is made at home. The alcohol is repeatedly passed through a filter covered with the ingredients, whether herbs or spices, until a highly concentrated extract has been achieved. An extract obtained in this manner is called a 'tincture', because it takes on not only the flavour and aroma of the ingredients but also their colour.

INFUSION

Also called maceration, this method is similar to the process of making tea, but using a mixture of alcohol and cold water. Herbs are left in the alcohol for a certain length of time to produce an extract that's again called a tincture, as it also takes on the flavours, aromas and colour of the ingredients. For example, green tea leaves are macerated to make a green tea liqueur.

BLENDING

The final part of the liqueur production process, in which the component parts are mixed with other ingredients – alcohol, water and possibly sugar – is called 'blending'. After this a period of rest is required to allow the liquid's ingredients to harmonise and develop.

▶ Modern stills come in many sizes and some are even portable, this one is heated using bottled gas.

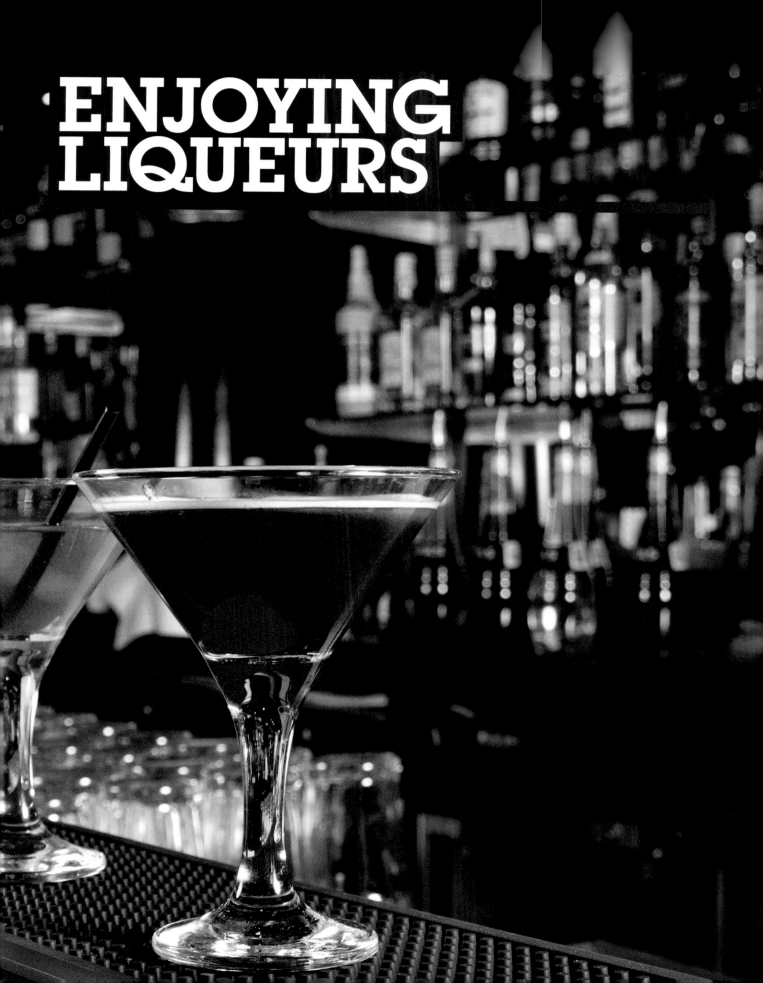

ENJOYING LIQUEURS

A Definition

So what are liqueurs? For most of us they're spirits that have been flavoured and sweetened. However, for anyone making liqueurs commercially there are more specific requirements.

▲ The addition of sugar is essential to creating a liqueur. The amount of sugar which can be added to commercial brands is prescribed by legislation.

According to United States law a liqueurs are a 'flavoured spirits product containing not less than 2½% by weight sugar, dextrose, levulose or a combination thereof made by mixing or redistilling any class or type of spirits with or over fruits, flowers, plants or pure juices therefrom or other natural flavoring materials or with extracts derived from infusions, percolation or maceration of such material'.

Similarly, most liqueurs produced in the European Union are required to have a minimum invert sugar content of 100g per litre. Other sugars can also be used, but the level of sweetness must be the equivalent of at least 100g of invert sugar per litre. Of course, most of us will use household sugar to make our own infusions, and won't have the faintest idea

what invert sugar is. 'Is it sugar that's upside down?' No. Invert sugar is a mixture of glucose and fructose that's obtained by splitting sucrose into these two components. Compared to sucrose, inverted sugar is sweeter, and its components – glucose and fructose – tend to retain moisture and are less prone to crystallisation.

A cherry liqueur has to have 70g of invert sugar and the alcohol must be cherry spirit. And should you want to make gentian or something similar using the plant's flowers or roots, then 80g of invert sugar per litre is needed. The minimum alcoholic strength by volume of liqueur should be 15% ABV. In addition, there are rules regarding the amount of egg and cream that can be used in a liqueur.

How to taste a liqueur

In the world of alcoholic drinks, liqueurs are something different. The range and vibrancy of the colours are suggestive of what's to come – and these can be all created in your own home.

Some liqueurs might have their origins in medicinal recipes created long ago, others will use exotic ingredients from faraway places but these days sourced mostly from supermarkets, while some of your finest creations might be produced from humble fruits picked in your own garden. There's seemingly no end to the magical colours, aromas, tastes and mouthfeels that can be created. Consequently there has to be a taste that suits everyone. Some are sweet others dry and herbal, many exude the flavour of summer fruits while others are redolent with cream and egg. But they all share one thing in common – they contain strong alcohol, usually around 40%, and deserve to be treated with respect.

A well-trained palate, time and a little knowledge are all key to unlocking the conundrum of what is in a glass. Like a famed masterpiece in an art gallery, a liqueur deserves to be given a little time and thought.

The Greek philosopher Aristotle said: 'The whole is greater than the sum of its parts.' And so it is with a liqueur. Appreciate its colour and aroma, taste the ingredients, picture their provenance, and the sum of all those parts will add to your enjoyment of the drink.

▶ Whisky liqueurs are stored in oak barrels before the sugar and other flavourings are added.

▼ Oak wood, peat, barley, vanilla, cloves and alcohol derived from potatoes all contribute to the character of liqueurs.

GLASS CLASS

A good drink is best enjoyed in a glass that maximises its taste, smell and appearance. Liqueurs are meant for sipping, not gulping, so a small glass is best. Liqueur glasses are usually smaller than a wine goblet and often made of delicate glass. They might have a stem or be a shot glass with no stem at all. The mood of the moment can be set by the style of glass you choose. Remember, these are drinks of elegance, so style and grace are everything.

USING YOUR EYES

From clear to iridescent green, jet black to a silky smooth silver cream, a liqueur can come in every colour of the rainbow. So inspect it carefully. Is it hazy or crystal clear? Tip and gently swirl the glass and let the liqueur coat its surface. This will help release some of its complex aromas. Watch and wait as the liquid runs back down the side of the glass – this is known as the 'legs' of the drink. Liqueurs by their nature are viscous and you should expect to see the drink flow slowly as it recedes down the side.

USING YOUR NOSE

Slowly, carefully breathe in the aroma of the liqueur. Savour the moment. Recent research has shown that our noses can detect and discriminate up to a trillion aromas, so it picks up many more tastes than our tongue can detect. Does your nose tell you the drink is too fruity or too spicy? Does the smell evoke any memories? Perhaps there's a hint of aniseed that evokes recollections of Greece. Is there a smell of fresh mint and cream, with its promise of a summer's day? So for just a moment resist taking a sip and let the liqueur's aromas swirl and your nose do its work.

TASTE TOUR

Take a small sip. What does it feel like in your mouth? Is it sweet, if so how sweet? Does it seem to stick to the inside of your mouth? Spread around your mouth is an array of sensitive taste buds that can detect saltiness, sweetness, bitterness, sourness and umami (savouriness). What flavours can you detect? Perhaps there are different fruits, or notes of vanilla or other spices. Is the mouthfeel light or heavy, smooth or firm? And once you swallow, is the finish long – does it make you want to take a second sip? Above all take your time. A drink deserves to be appreciated and treated with respect.

Some facts about liqueurs

- A liqueur is an alcoholic drink made from a distilled spirit that's been flavoured with fruit, cream, herbs, spices, flowers or nuts and bottled with added sugar or another sweetener.
- In parts of the United States, liqueurs may also be called cordials or schnapps.
- In the US, 16 October is recognised as National Liqueur Day, which celebrates the countless types and flavours of liqueur.
- The word liqueur comes from the Latin word *liquifacere*, meaning to liquefy.
- All liqueurs are blends.
- Sloe gin isn't gin at all but a liqueur.
- Liqueurs aren't usually aged for any great length of time, although their base spirit, such as whisky, could be.
- Distilled spirits don't contain any cholesterol, carbohydrates or fats of any kind.
- Most vegetables and almost all fruits naturally contain a small amount of alcohol.
- Liqueurs can be drunk neat, poured over ice, or combined with cream and other mixers to create cocktails. They're often served with or after a dessert. They can also be also used in cooking.
- Many present-day liqueurs are the historical descendants of herbal medicines.

An A-Z of commercial liqueurs

A staggering variety of liqueurs are now produced worldwide, from everyday flavours such as coffee and vanilla found in most kitchens, to the more esoteric delights of central American desert plants and Japanese plums. Commercial liqueurs are the base for some of the world's greatest cocktails or are pleasing just to drink on their own. With a little bit of practice you'll find that you can make your own versions of many of these classic drinks.

Abisante

Pale green, aniseed-flavoured liqueur. It can be used as an alternative to absinthe. However, it doesn't contain wormwood, the woody shrub with a bitter aromatic taste that's used as an ingredient of absinthe.

Absinthe

An aniseed-flavoured liqueur that has a reputation for being hallucinogenic, which resulted in its sale being banned in some countries. However, it's no more likely to make a drinker see things than any other spirit. Its flavour primarily comes from the leaves and flowers of wormwood. Other ingredients include green anise and sweet fennel. Traditionally the drink has a green colour but it may also be colourless.

Advocaat

A Christmas favourite from Holland that's made of egg yolks, brandy, sugar and vanilla. It looks and tastes like a rich, alcoholic creamy custard. It's often called eggnog.

Agavero

A tequila-flavoured liqueur from Mexico. It's made using a blend of blue agave reposado and anejo tequilas, which are aged in white oak casks. The drink is flavoured with flowers from the damiana, a commonly occurring shrub in Central America and southern US states. The plant is believed by some to be an aphrodisiac.

Amaretto

An almond-flavoured liqueur made with apricots or almonds. It originates from Saronno in Italy, its name being derived from the Italian word for bitter.

Amaro Meletti

A bitter Italian digestif flavoured with various aromatic herbs including aniseed and saffron. Developed in 1870 by Silvio Meletti, who refined a recipe made by his mother.

Amer Picon

A bitter orange French aperitif. Created in the 1830s, it contains essences of gentian and quinine.

Aperol

An Italian aperitif produced from a recipe developed in 1919. Orange in colour and flavour, it also includes rhubarb, chinchona and genziana along with other secret ingredients.

Bärenjäger

A very sweet, honey-flavoured liqueur probably first made in the 15th century in what is now Germany. Also known as Bärenfang, which means 'bear trap', it derives from vodka.

Benedictine

A herb-flavoured brandy-based liqueur. After World War One Benedictine was particularly popular in working men's clubs in Lancashire. It is said that soldiers from Lancashire had acquired a taste for it while they were stationed in France during the war. It is often served with a whisky or a cognac in a cocktail.

(Courtesy Benedictine)

Calvados

An apple brandy, distilled from cider, speciality of the Normandy region of France where is has been made at least since the 1500s, perhaps going as far back as Charlemagne. It is usually made from apples but sometimes of pears and is matured in wooden casks, often for several years.

Campari

A famous Italian aperitif derived from peppers, oranges and other herbs and spices. The recipe was originally developed by Gaspare Campari in 1860 for his Cafe Campari in Milan. It's often mixed with lemonade.

Chambord

A liqueur that dates back to 1685. According to legend it was developed when Louis XIV visited Château de Chambord in the Loire valley in France. It's made from red and black raspberries, citrus peel, honey, vanilla and brandy.

Chartreuse

A bright, naturally green herbal and brandy-based liqueur, made with more than 130 different ingredients and aged in oak casks. A yellow version is also made.

Cherry Heering

A naturally flavoured cherry liqueur from Denmark that's used in a variety of cocktails. The ruby-red liqueur is made by soaking lightly crushed Danish cherries and a blend of spices in neutral grain spirits. It's then cask-matured for up to five years, with sugar added during the ageing process.

(Courtesy of Heering)

Cointreau

An orange-flavoured liqueur, or triple sec, made in France and Spain from dried bitter orange peel and sweet orange peel.

Crème de café

A coffee-flavoured liqueur. The most popular coffee liqueurs are the Mexican kahlúa, Tia Maria from Jamaica and Pasha from Turkey.

Crème de cassis

A sweet, low-strength liqueur made from French blackcurrants. Used for several cocktails, including the very popular kir.

Crème de menthe

A sweet liqueur flavoured with mint leaves. It can be either clear or green.

Crème de noyaux

A pink liqueur with a distinct almond flavour. Made from the stones of plums, cherries, peaches and apricots.

Curaçao

Made of the dried peels of bitter laraha oranges grown on the island of Curaçao Curaçao. Usually it's orange in colour, but white, blue and green variants are also produced.

Cynar

A quinine-flavoured drink made from artichokes.

Domaine de Canton

A modern ginger-flavoured liqueur developed in 2007, made with a mixture of eau-de-vie and cognac.

Drambuie

A liqueur that is a blend of Scottish whisky, heather honey and herbs. The name comes from the Gaelic phrase *dram buidheach*, 'the drink that satisfies'.

Dubonnet rouge

A bitter, wine-based vermouth liqueur made from three varieties of Muscat grapes and flavoured with quinine and bitter bark.

Fernet-branca

A bitter herbal digestif made with a recipe that includes more than 40 herbs, roots and spices. It has a pronounced menthol-eucalyptus flavour.

Frangelico

This nutty, hazelnut-flavoured liqueur is made from the infusion of toasted hazelnuts. Other flavours come from roasted coffee grains, cocoa, vanilla berries and rhubarb.

Galliano

A spicy herbal-based liqueur made in Italy. It has an aniseed and vanilla flavour derived from herbs and spices.

Goldschlager

A Swiss, clear-coloured cinnamon schnapps that contains small gold leaf flakes.

Grand Marnier

A curaçao orange liqueur from France with a cognac or brandy base.

Herbsaint

An aniseed-flavoured liqueur, similar to absinthe.

Hpnotiq

A blue blend of fruit juice, vodka and cognac.

Irish cream liqueur

A creamy liqueur made of Irish whiskey, cream and sometimes chocolate. Baileys is one of the most famous labels. It is used in many cocktails and is often seen as a Christmas drink.

Irish Mist

A sweet, aromatic blend of Irish whiskey, honey and herbs.

Irish velvet

A coffee liqueur made from Irish whiskey, black coffee and sugar.

Jägermeister

A dark red herbal liqueur from Germany, made from 56 herbs and spices, that has enjoyed a recent rise in popularity outside its country of origin. A favourite with people who like to drink shots.

Licor 43

A golden Spanish liqueur made, unsurprisingly, from 43 Mediterranean citrus fruits and select herbs and spices.

(Cath Harries)

Limoncello

A sweet, lemon-flavoured Italian dessert liqueur made from lemon zests.

Maraschino

A clear, dry, cherry-flavoured liqueur made from the Marasca cherries and kernels.

Midori

A bright green-coloured liqueur that has a sweet melon flavour.

Ouzo

A clear, distilled wine that's flavoured with aniseed and other herbs from Greece. When water is added it turns cloudy.

Peppermint schnapps

Similar to crème de menthe, but uses less sugar and more alcohol. Has a strong, snappy mint flavour and is often used in winter cocktails.

Pimento Dram

A rum liqueur made in Jamaica. Based on allspice and includes cloves, nutmeg and cinnamon.

Pimm's

A spirit-based summer cocktail mixer served in tall glasses with cucumber and fruit, ice and lemonade or ginger ale. The most popular is Pimm's No 1 Cup, which is gin-based. There are rum, whisky, vodka and brandy variants.

Raki

A spirit from, usually, Turkey, similar to ouzo. Flavoured with aniseed and liquorice.

Sambuca

An Italian liqueur made from the oils of anise, star anise, liquorice, elderflower and other spices. In bars it is often lit and served to the customer still flaming.

Schnapps

A distilled spirit that is usually produced with fruit in the fermentation. Schnapps comes in many flavours including apple, cinnamon and peppermint.

Somrus

An Indian cream liqueur made from a blend of rum, dairy cream and spices.

Southern Comfort

An American liqueur made from a whiskey base flavoured with peaches.

Strega

An Italian liqueur made of 70 herbs and spices including mint, cinnamon, juniper, saffron, fennel and iris. It has a distinct yellow colour. Strega is the Italian word for 'witch'.

Triple sec

An orange-flavoured liqueur, but often used as a generic name for all orange liqueurs. It's often very sweet. Cointreau is one of the most famous brands of triple sec.

Tuaca

A brandy liqueur flavoured with citrus and vanilla originally produced by the Tuoni and Canepa families from Livorno, Italy.

Ty Ku

A light green liqueur with a sake and Asian vodka base. The flavour is derived from 20 different fruits including pomegranate, ginseng and damiana.

Unicum

A bitter, herbal digestif from Hungary, today produced by Zwack, made with 40 herbs and spices.

X-Rated Fusion

A pink liqueur from France that infuses mango, Provence blood oranges and passion fruit in premium vodka.

MAKING LIQUEURS

Home infusing

Making infusions and liqueurs is easy, and the ingredients are so simple: the material to be infused – it could be fruit, flowers, nuts, herbs, spices, sweets or even meat; a spirit – *any* spirit, such as vodka, gin or whisky, though many infusers prefer to use vodka because of its relatively neutral taste; and sugar – an optional ingredient. Once you've mastered the technique – little more than pouring, steeping, waiting and straining – you've opened the door to a whole new world of flavoured drinks, and a little practice will soon enable you to adjust your recipes to produce the exact flavours you want.

GETTING SWEET ON SUGAR SYRUP

Many traditional recipes that add sugar to infusions – thereby making them liqueurs – advise adding granulated sugar at the start of the infusion process. And indeed, perfectly acceptable liqueurs can be made doing it this way. But they'll probably take longer to be ready to drink, as you have to wait for the sugar to properly dissolve. Also, it's hard to control the level of sweetness – if your sugared infusion is too sweet, it's very difficult to take that sweetness out. So contrary to popular belief there's very little point in adding sugar at the outset, not least because saturating the spirit with sugar prevents it from extracting the natural fruit sugars and flavours from the ingredients you are using.

Over time I've learnt that one of the common complaints about many recipes is that some years they produce a liqueur that's too sweet, while other years they're not sweet enough. But sweetening to taste at the end of the maceration process yields a perfect batch every time. If you use simple syrup instead of granulated sugar you don't have to wait for the crystals to dissolve. Sugar syrup also helps improve the mouthfeel of an infusion.

The best way to solve this problem is to produce your own sugar syrup – it's easy, and it can be kept in the fridge ready for when it is needed. When you come to use it add only a little at first, as you sometimes require only a fraction of the quantity called for in many traditional recipes.

Note that brown sugar is used for sugar syrup when masking a brandy or whisky-based infusion. Honey can also be used to sweeten a liqueur, but its taste can be quite strong, so use it sparingly.

Sugar syrup recipe

1 Combine equal measures of sugar and water in a saucepan over low heat – one cup/mug of sugar to one cup/mug of tap water.

2 Warm the mixture until the sugar dissolves, then allow it to cool.

3 If you prefer a higher strength, it's possible to make syrup with three parts sugar and two parts water, to reduce dilution of the spirit.

(Cath Harries)

▶ A supply of good quality glass jars are essential for the serious home infuser.

EQUIPMENT

Making flavoured spirits requires very little in the way of equipment – principally a Kilner jar and not much else. My own preference is for smaller-sized jars, especially if I'm trying an ingredient for the first time. Then I can use about 250ml of my chosen spirit for each infusion, and if something works it's very easy to scale up to larger volumes; and if it doesn't work not much has been lost.

Most of the equipment you'll need will be readily found in all functional kitchens:

■ Weighing scales
■ Measuring jug
■ Containers to infuse in (Kilner jars or similar; Kilner jars have a nice wide top, enabling ingredients to be easily added).
■ Saucepan
■ Knives
■ Funnel
■ Coffee or wine filters
■ Glass bottles in which to keep the infusion; these can be sealed with a screw cap or cork.
■ Labels. It's always sensible to label bottle and jars; ideally your labels should provide details of the content and the date of infusion or bottling.

INGREDIENTS

The ingredients you use in your liqueurs are limited only by your imagination and the flavour that you want to create.

■ **Fresh ripe fruit** – Full of natural goodness and sugars. Use only the best fruit and avoid bruised or damaged material.
■ **Frozen fruit** – A good way of preserving fruit. Freezing breaks down the fruit's cell walls, which makes it easier for juices to be released into the infusing spirit.
■ **Wild fruit** – One of the joys of infusing is using wild fruits that you've foraged.

▲ A modest herb garden at home will include many plants suitable for infusions. The fun is in experimenting.

▼ Some infusers prefer to add granulated sugar rather than sugar syrup to their creations.

■ **Dry fruit** – Full of sweet flavours, but very little moisture. They'll usually produce a clear liqueur.

■ **Fruit with stones** – Most stones or pits are best discarded. However, the presence of a small number can add to the depth of flavour of a drink.

■ **Fruit with seeds** – Seeds can add bitterness to the final infusion and ideally should be removed.

■ **Fresh herbs** – Adding spirit to fresh herbs will help release their oils and flavours.

■ **Floral infusions** – Quick and easy to make, you don't normally need to add sugar unless you like your drinks a little sweeter. Ensure that the flowers you choose aren't toxic! Some garden plants, such as daffodils, are poisonous, as are some wild flowers.

■ **Nut infusions** – It's always best to crush the nuts, but don't turn them into a flour, which can lead to a cloudy infusion. However, given time – possibly several months – the clouding will settle.

■ **Sweets** – Sugar-based sweets such as Skittles will dissolve in a spirit. They can quickly produce a vivid coloured infusion.

GENERAL PRINCIPLES FOR THE HOME INFUSER

Adding fruit to a spirit to get an infusion isn't a precise science, but in general the stronger the flavour of the ingredients the shorter the time needed for an infusion to develop. The tip is to keep tasting the infusion. When you're happy with it, simply strain and bottle.

▲ **When bottled, homemade infusions make ideal Christmas and birthday presents.**

(Cath Harries)

Adding the ingredients

A rough guide regarding the quantity of ingredients you should add is a small handful for every 250ml of spirit, and a good handful to a full bottle of spirit (750 ml).

Straining and filtering

Some liqueurs just need straining when you are bottling, simply pour the liquid through a metal sieve. When straining the ingredients avoid pressing all the liquid out, particularly from fruit. You might get more liquid, but there's a danger of making the infusion cloudy in the process. If after sieving, however, your liqueur still has small particles floating around, or looks cloudy, it is a good idea to filter it to keep the flavour and appearance clear and pure. Filtering can be done through a piece of muslin or cheesecloth within a sieve, or through a coffee filter lined with a double paper cone. Keep a filter cone that is dedicated to your infusions, don't use one that has also been used for making coffee. The leftover fruit pulp can be used as a spirit-infused dessert.

Cleanliness

All your equipment should be clean and dry, but nothing needs to be sterilised. In addition you should always wash and prepare your ingredients before adding them to the spirit.

Maceration

Leave the Kilner jars in a dark, cool place. Don't be afraid to have a taste during the maceration process.

Amount to make

Most recipes call for approximately 750ml of a spirit or 250ml. My tip is don't make too much. Small amounts, rather than a whole bottle, are often better. If I'm experimenting with new ingredients I'll start with about 250/350ml of spirit. This allows me to experiment far more, and means that in the unlikely event of something going wrong relatively little is wasted.

Time is of the essence

There's no perfect length of time for making an infusion – it could take moments or weeks. Steeping fruit in alcohol for longer periods doesn't always improve the flavour. So, don't be afraid to taste an infusion; when you think it's ready, it probably is. It might not be sweet enough for your personal taste, but I prefer to add sugar syrup after infusing. It's a quicker way of making an infusion than putting in granulated sugar at the start of the process. Waiting for the sugar to dissolve takes ages.

▼ **The zest of an orange can transform the humblest white spirit into a drink of some allure.** (Cath Harries)

▼ **Don't' throw away the strained fruit from your infusions – it can be used as an ingredient for a boozy dessert.** (Cath Harries)

▼ **Infusions do not have to be made in large quantities, 250-300ml of spirit works fine.** (Cath Harries)

Timing

- Hot chillies, cardamom and citrus fruits such as lemons or oranges could all be ready for consumption within a day, but a few days is more likely. Dry, hard ingredients, such as spices, will take longer.
- Most infusions will last for a long time, and many improve with age.
- Ripe ingredients such as cherries require shorter steep times. Often 24 hours will be enough. If you have doubts about how strong the flavours will be, add only small amounts of the ingredients at first. Steep for 24 hours, then, if the taste isn't strong enough, add another handful of the ingredients and steep for another 24 hours.
- Putting the infusion in a fridge will slow the infusion time.

Bottling it up

It is best to keep the infusion in a tightly closed container (to prevent oxidation), stored in a dark, cool, room-temperature place such as a cupboard. There are plenty of examples of long-forgotten bottles of sloe gin being discovered at the back of a cupboard shelf and still being palatable, despite being years old. Once the bottle has been opened the liquid comes in touch with air, and this can cause oxidation. However, it should last, without much change to the taste, for at least six months. Cream and egg liqueurs aren't as resilient. Once opened they're probably best kept in a fridge and drunk within a couple of months.

Keep records

Simple notes on the contents of each infusion are useful to have, especially when you want to recreate something made years earlier.

▼ Home infusers get used to having many jars with different ingredients in their cupboards. (Cath Harries)

Don't be afraid to experiment

One of the bonuses of making infusions in small batches is that it is easy to experiment with new ingredients or combinations. If you think chilli, cucumber and fresh ginger sounds an interesting combination, then give it a go. If you see an unusual fruit in the market, then buy a few and see how they work in an infusion.

Infusion or liqueur?

All liqueurs are infusions, but not all infusions are liqueurs. If the infused or macerated ingredients have sugar added to them, it's a liqueur. If no sugar is used, then it's an infusion.

What spirit to use?

Most infusers use vodka or gin (especially vodka), but any other spirit can be used. For beginners a clear spirit is probably best, and vodka is the alcohol of choice for most because of its relatively neutral taste. However, gin, white rum or other clear spirits can be used. Just be aware of the flavourings already in the drink.

If you're infusing with one of the stronger, more complex-tasting spirits, such as brandy or whisky, then it's probably best to use ingredients with stronger compatible flavours. Many infusers make very successful infusions using such spirits, and with practice you'll find out what works best for you when using them.

HOW STRONG ARE MY INFUSIONS?

Well, if you start off with 40% ABV (alcohol by volume), then you'll still have 40% alcohol in your drink. It might have been diluted, true – liquid could have come out of the fruit you're infusing – and you might have added sugar syrup or cream to the infusion, which will also have increased the dilution. But either way, you won't have increased the alcohol in the drink, as you aren't making new alcohol through fermentation.

For example, if you take a litre of spirit with a 50% ABV it's 50% alcohol and 50% water, which means that there are 500ml of alcohol in it, and if you add a further litre of water the ABV is reduced down to 25%; however, there are still 500ml of alcohol in the resultant drink, it's just less concentrated.

So if you start off with a litre of spirit at 40% ABV, which is the most common strength, it contains 400ml of alcohol. If you add in a litre of water or other liquid the ABV is reduced down to 20%. However, as before, there will still be 400ml of alcohol in it.

In the US alcoholic content of a drink is often measured as alcohol proof. An American whiskey or vodka will often state '80 proof'. But this doesn't mean that it's twice as strong as a Scotch whisky – in the US alcohol proof is defined as twice the percentage of alcohol by volume, so a 120 proof spirit has an ABV of 60%, 80 proof is 40% ABV, and so on.

It is thought that the original term 'proof' dates back to 16th century England, when spirits were taxed at different rates depending on their alcohol content. At that date the alcohol content of spirits was determined by using gunpowder, and a sample was 'proved' acceptable by pouring some of it on gunpowder and lighting it. If it burned steadily with a blue flame it was considered 100 degrees 'proof', and equalled 57.15% alcohol. If it failed to burn, it was considered 'underproof', and if it burned too quickly it was 'overproof'. At some point the 57.15% was adjusted to 50%, to make life a little easier.

THE BEST SPIRITS TO BUY

So what are the best spirits to buy to make a liqueur or infusion? The most expensive, or the cheapest? Well, it really is a matter of taste, but a rule of thumb would be that if you like to drink it, then it is probably good enough to make your own liqueurs and infusions from.

Ideally it is best to have a neutral-flavoured spirit that is clean-tasting and uncomplicated. Some gins are often jam-packed with botanical flavours, including juniper, coriander and cardamom, which may overpower or clash with your ingredient. So try to use an ingredient that'll work in harmony with the underlying characteristic of your chosen spirit. Vodka will work with just about everything. Spiced rum is a little harder, but try it infused with some crushed, fresh mint leaves.

You certainly don't have to buy the most expensive spirits. You can save yourself a lot of money by using some of the own-label brands sold by supermarkets – you don't have to buy the big brands. Recently, supermarket gins from Morrisons, Lidl and Waitrose topped the *Which?* gin taste test. *Which?* editor Richard Headland said: 'Once again our taste tests have shown that supermarket own labels are giving the big brands a real run for their money. Some inexpensive bottles received a much higher score from our experts, proving you don't always need to splash out. ... Morrisons' London Dry Gin (£10.49) came top of the gin taste test with a score of 80%, with experts describing it as 'well-rounded' and 'refreshing'. Lidl's Castelgy

London Dry Gin was the joint-cheapest gin we tested, costing £9.99, and came joint-second in our test with Waitrose London Dry Gin (£12), both scoring 78%. Greenalls' London Dry Gin (£15) was the top scoring branded gin but was ranked fourth overall in our taste test, with a score of 77%. Gordon's Special Dry London Gin was ranked ninth with a score of 74%.' (The prices quoted here were correct at the time of the report, which was August 2015.) The own-labels fared equally well when it came to testing whiskies. For example, Aldi's Highland Black eight-year-old whisky was considered sophisticated, balanced, smooth and creamy.

However, some lower-priced vodkas might have a taste you don't like, and in some cases could dominate the flavour of your infusion. Ideally vodkas should be colourless, flavourless and odourless, and the very best are likely to have been distilled a number of times and then filtered through charcoal to remove unwanted flavours.

While most people won't be able to or want to distil something at home (which is illegal without a licence in the UK), it is possible to filter a spirit if you want to try and improve its flavour. If you have a water filter or something similar at home, then you can strip some of the flavour impurities out of the spirit you've bought. Just pour the vodka through the filter three or even four times and the taste should be improved. But be aware that once the filter element has had vodka passed through it it can't be used for water again, and will have to be replaced.

If you don't have a water filter you can still cleanse the vodka using activated charcoal, which you can buy from a

pet shop. Activated charcoal is widely used by people who own aquariums, to remove unwanted nasties from their piscatorial water. To cleanse vodka this way, all you need is some activated charcoal, a coffee filter and a funnel. Note that it's best to rinse the charcoal beforehand, to remove any dust. Then simply pour the vodka through the filter, collect it and repeat three or four times. Some proponents of filtering say it's best to chill the vodka before filtering.

TASTE TROUBLESHOOTING

Depending on what kind of flavouring you've used – and depending on the concentration of the constituents you've extracted – infusion is likely fall into one of the following categories:

■ 'I like that.'
■ 'Whoa, the flavour's too strong.'
■ 'It needs more taste.'

If it's either of the last two, all is not lost. You can do something about it.

If you're happy with the taste, filter through a cheesecloth-lined sieve or paper if necessary, and bottle carefully, ensuring the cap/cork is tightly in place, and ideally store in a dark place at room temperature. Remember – direct sunlight and excessive heat can change the flavour profile and colour of your creations.

And don't be too worried if it looks a little cloudy or a sediment forms at the bottom of the bottle. You can opt to do nothing about it – after all, it's a hand-crafted drink and a little cloudiness won't do any harm – but if it bothers you just filter it again.

If the flavour is too strong, add a little more of your base spirit until you achieve the taste you want. Forget about it for a week or so and then taste it again.

If, on the other hand, there's not enough taste, add a little more sugar syrup. However, if you want to make a commercial liqueur remember that there are rules regarding the number of grams of sugar per litre. These rules don't apply to home infusions. Adding the sugar as a simple syrup will mean that the sweetness dissipates into the drink much faster than if solid sugar was used.

If you're still not happy, put the liqueur into a cupboard and leave it for a couple of months. You might be quite surprised how much you like it after it's aged a bit.

WHAT YOU CAN INFUSE

The only limit is your imagination. The fun is in *experimenting*, not just with one ingredient but also with combinations of different ingredients. Think of yourself as the conductor of an orchestra and the ingredients as your instruments. Experiment with different ingredients, but always remember to keep sampling the infusion and to keep notes. And remember, if you've chopped the ingredients very fine you'll have to be prepared to filter it several times through a cheesecloth-lined sieve, or filter paper, if you want an ultra-clear infusion.

A little bit of science

Maceration is the classic method of making an infusion. And it's easy. It's as simple as steeping (soaking) a fruit, herb, spice or even a slice of bacon in alcohol and then letting it sit in a container for a few hours, days or even months. You don't have to do much more than shake the container every now and again. With maceration the alcohol becomes intensely flavoured, raising it to a different level.

And while it isn't necessary, it's useful to understand a little bit of the science behind what's going on. In fact two processes are occurring when you infuse your ingredients in alcohol: osmosis and dissolution.

Osmosis is nature's attempt to achieve balance. Essentially fresh ingredients such as fruit and vegetables contain a lot of water and a lot less alcohol. So the water from the fruit flows out to the place where there's less water – the alcohol. This process continues until there's a balance.

Some of you might remember this from when you did chemistry at school. In chemistry, a solution is a mixture of one substance dissolved in another. The substance that does the dissolving is called the solvent and the substance that's dissolved is called the solute. So when infusing some fruit, such as

a strawberry, the solute is alcohol, the solvent is the water within the strawberry, and the semipermeable membrane is the cellular walls of the strawberry. When the strawberry is coated in alcohol there's a much higher concentration of solute outside it than inside it. This causes our solvent (water) to flow out of the fruit and into the surrounding environment in an attempt to equalise the concentration on both sides.

In its simplest form infusion of a liquid is affected by the size of the ingredients, their weight, pressure and temperature of the ingredient to be infused, and alcohol content. However, for home infusers the two most important aspects are probably the size of the ingredients and how much you're using.

As a general rule chopping, crushing or breaking up the ingredients to a smaller size will make them infuse faster. The more an ingredient is broken up, the less of it will be required.

The second process, dissolution, happens when dried flavourings have no water to be exchanged, so the process is about releasing and dissolving compounds into the alcohol. For alcohol to be more effective it needs to be a high concentration, at least 40% ABV. This alcohol strength is that found in most spirits sold commercially.

Foraging

Foraging is the age-old process of gathering food from nature, and one of my childhood memories is of my parents going foraging. Blackberries, nettles, sloes – seemingly whatever was in season was picked. Indeed, anything growing by the roadside or in a wood was fair game. For them the development of Tupperware containers must have seemed like a huge leap forward in terms of technology. At last they had something robust in which to gather nature's bounty without the risk of it getting squashed!

Foraging is a practice that for a while seemed to have fallen out of fashion, and the convenience of the supermarket reigned supreme. However, today a new generation has started to seek out food that's growing wild. There are over 20,000 species of plants that have been recorded as edible, but you'll be lucky to find more than 25 of them in your local supermarket. Foraged plants are consequently a great addition to a healthy, balanced lifestyle. And most can be used in infusions too. If you're lucky they'll be available locally, are sustainable so long as you're not greedy, and are free. They're also fun to find. Just be sure you don't trespass.

The use of locally-sourced herbs and fruits is becoming a widespread phenomenon. The flavours, textures and nutrients from foraged fruits are elemental and vital, and can add a new

dimension to your home infusing. And foraging for them will bring you closer to nature and the changing rhythms of the seasons.

It wasn't long ago that gathering wild food was a normal part of British culture – during World War Two rose hips were commercially gathered because of their high vitamin C content. And now we're seeing a real food renaissance, including a resurgence in the number of allotment holders, people growing their own food at home, and more and more people interested in foraging and wild food.

Spring is a good time to start. The lush growth of summer hasn't begun and there are a few easily identified plants about to get you started. From there on follow the seasons. Almost the whole year around, in woodlands, fields and hedgerows, and springing from cracks in trees, you can find a surprising range of material for infusion.

But remember, nothing is really for free. The cost of over-foraging can be serious damage to the environment. And remember too that if you can't identify accurately what you're picking, it's best to leave it where it is.

▲▼ Some poisonous berries look very innocent and edible, these pokeberries (above) look very similar to blackcurrants or bilberries (below) but are in fact deadly to humans. Even though birds and animals can eat them safely a small handful would be fatal to a child.

Edible flowers

As well as berries, fruits and nuts, infusions can also be made from edible flowers, of which there are hundreds including rose petals, violets, bergamot, chrysanthemums, marigolds and elderflowers. However, it's always best to check whether a plant is edible before you try it – a bloom might look good and smell good, but it could nevertheless be poisonous. Also, be aware that picking many wild flowers in the UK is illegal due to their rarity, so always check the plant's legal status before you take them.

If you're only using flower petals or fresh herbs, don't infuse the cordial for the several weeks that fruit options require: two days should be more than enough to draw out their flavour without any bitterness.

Edible garden flowers include:

- **Begonia** – Begonia blossoms have a citrus-sour taste.
- **Marigold** – Flavours range from spicy to bitter, tangy to peppery.
- **Carnation** – One of the secret ingredients of Chartreuse.
- **Clover** – Sweet, anise-like and liquorice flavours.
- **Cornflower** – Slightly sweet and spicy.
- **Dandelion** – Young flowers have a honey-like flavour. Mature flowers are bitter.
- **Elderflower** – Sweet to smell and have a sweet taste.
- **Hibiscus** – Has a cranberry-like flavour with citrus overtones.
- **Nasturtium** – Flowers have a sweet, spicy flavour.
- **Rose** – Flavours include strawberries and green apples, with overtones of sweetness.
- **Sweet violet** – Delicate, fragrant flavours.

Edible herb flowers include:

- **Angelica** – Its flavour is similar to liquorice.
- **Hyssop** – The flowers and leaves have a delicate anise or liquorice flavour.
- **Basil** – A variety of flavours, from lemon to mint.
- **Bergamot** – Aromatic lemon and orange flavours.
- **Borage** – A faint taste of cucumber.
- **Burnet** – Similar to borage, a subtle taste of cucumber.
- **Chervil** – Subtle flavour of anise.
- **Chicory** – Earthy, bitter flavour.
- **Coriander** – Strong, warm flavour of spice.
- **Fennel** – Has a mild anise flavour.
- **Ginger** – Unsurprisingly, tastes of ginger.
- **Jasmine** – Fragrant, floral notes, highly aromatic.
- **Lavender** – Notes of lemon and citrus.
- **Lemon verbena** – Delicate orange and lemon citrus flavours.

Natural flavour combinations

Some of the best infusions are often made with more than one fruit or a combination of herbs and spices. Plums, cherries, strawberries, raspberries, currants, blackberries, blueberries, peaches, apples, apricots – in fact any fruit can be used. You can experiment with whatever is in season or on sale at a local supermarket. The mix is up to you, but take care not to mix fruits that have very strong flavours. Tried and trusted flavour pairings include:

- Apple and cinnamon
- Blackcurrant and rosemary
- Raspberry and lemon balm
- Strawberry and basil
- Peach and ginger
- Pineapple and basil
- Strawberry and mint
- Orange and coffee beans

A forager and gardener's calendar

So, what should you look for and when? There's always something that can be found in gardens or out on walks from which an infusion can be made. However, if you can't find anything just head off to the supermarket. Needless to say, there are many more fruits and flowers suitable for infusions than can be listed here.

	Jan	Feb	Mar	Apr	May	Jun	Jul	Aug	Sep	Oct	Nov	Dec
Alexanders			•	•	•	•					•	•
Apricot							•	•				
Basil					•	•	•	•	•			
Bilberry							•	•	•	•		
Blackberry					•	•	•	•	•	•		
Blackcurrant							•	•	•			
Cherry						•	•					
Chestnut										•	•	
Chilli							•	•	•			
Coriander						•	•	•				
Crab apple									•	•		
Damson									•	•		
Dandelion			•	•	•							
Elderberry								•				
Elderflower						•	•					
Fennel					•	•						
Gorse flower				•								
Haw								•	•	•	•	•
Mint				•	•	•	•	•	•	•	•	
Nettle					•	•						
Plum								•	•	•		
Raspberry							•	•	•			
Rhubarb			•	•	•	•	•					
Rose hip									•	•	•	•
Rose petal						•	•	•				
Sage					•	•						
Sea buckthorn							•	•	•	•	•	
Sloe										•	•	•
Strawberry						•	•	•				
Walnut						•	•					
Wormwood					•	•	•	•	•			

Going seasonal

One of the joys of making infusions is using fresh, seasonal ingredients. It's often worthwhile walking through a farmers' market to find out which fruits and vegetables are at their peak. That way you can often find fruits, vegetables and herbs or spices that you might not have considered before, and then make an infusion from them when you get home.

Commonly available herbs that can be found in your own garden include rosemary, sage, garlic and mint. As a general rule of thumb, if it's edible it can be used in an infusion. The more you experiment, the more fun it is. You're less likely to find fruit in your garden, unless you've planted it yourself, but what you don't have growing you can get in your local greengrocers, supermarket or farmers' market: strawberries, raspberries, cherries, oranges, lemons and even coconut are all valid candidates. And don't forget your vegetable patch and what's growing in or around the greenhouse. Garlic, chilli and fennel all make fabulous infusions.

The spice rack in your kitchen can also be a source of inspiration – for instance, cardamom, ginger and vanilla pods can all make a creative contribution to infusions. And don't forget to look in the fridge, where some lemon grass or other potential ingredients could be waiting to be used.

Just be aware that the more of an ingredient you add, the stronger the flavour of the infusion will be. So it would be better to start with two chillies rather than ten. As a rule of thumb, 150–300g of ingredients per 750ml of spirit will be fine. If making a smaller quantity, or experimenting, then 50–100g for each 250ml of spirit is about right.

CHAPTER 5
SIGNIFICANT INFUSIONS

Understanding the spirit world

When you are starting out as an infuser of spirits it is important that you understand the spirits you will be working with, or attempting to reproduce.

GIN, THE ULTIMATE INFUSED SPIRIT

When it comes to flavoured spirits, gin has to be one of the best known. Its essential flavouring ingredient is the aromatic fruit of the evergreen juniper bush. Other ingredients comprise assorted botanicals and spices that can include cardamom and coriander.

Each distillery has its own ingredients, which often includes angelica, orris root, orange peel, lemon peel – in fact the list of botanicals is seemingly endless and more than 100 have been identified. Some gin makers infuse with almonds, blackcurrant, ginger, nutmeg and even coconut. Consequently gins can variously taste spicy, fruity and even sweet. Needless to say, gin distillers usually guard their recipes very carefully. The proportions of the botanicals used is the determining factor in the taste and character of each gin. The aim is to make a balanced, complex drink.

Most gin is assembled or compounded rather than distilled. This involves taking a neutral very strong spirit – which could be made from grain or molasses and is about 80% ABV – diluting it to about 60% ABV and putting it into what's usually called a carter head pot still, with a number of flavouring botanicals.

An alternative method of making gin is by cold compounding, which involves the blending together of the spirit and a macerated distillate of the botanicals. No ageing is needed – gin doesn't have to be aged for three years like whisky. Finally the spirit is diluted down to selling strength with distilled water to, usually, around 40% alcohol. It's then bottled and ready to sell.

Some of the most strongly flavoured gins are made by heating the spirit and allowing its steam to pass through the botanicals to absorb their aromas and tastes.

▼ A variety of botanicals are used to make gin, but expect juniper to be at the fore of the flavour.

The different processes of making gin give us its distinct styles. Probably the best known is London gin, as made at Sipsmith. The style is clean and dry with a clean flavour of juniper.

The history of gin is a long and illustrious one. Indeed, juniper-flavoured drinks became popular in Europe as far

▶▲◀ Many cocktail bars will make the own gin based fruit infusions, which they store in large jars. (Six Storeys on Soho)

▼ Many bartenders low to show off their mixology skills by making their own, unique infusions. (Six Storeys on Soho)

back as the 14th century, when some believed they helped relieve sickness and ward off the Black Death. But it is London that's considered to be the home of the spirit we know and love as gin.

It is thought that gin came to England in the 17th century after English troops fighting in support of the Dutch in the Eighty Years War got a taste for it – whence also its name, from the Dutch word for juniper (*genever*). It was soon after this that William II, Prince of Orange, and his protestant wife Mary, daughter of King Charles I, became the rulers of England, and discord between England and France led to the importation of brandy from Catholic countries being banned. The domestic production of spirits from other grains was therefore encouraged, leading to the development of the UK's whisky and gin industries. Today it's almost impossible to imagine the popularity of gin at that time. In 1733, at the height of the 'Gin Craze', more than 50 litres a year was being produced per resident of London.

LONDON GIN REVIVAL

The history of London's gin industry is peppered with tales of small-scale producers boiling up heady spirits in tiny sheds. So it was natural that the construction in 2009 of a new copper still in the capital, for the first time in 189 years, should occur in a tin-roofed suburban garage in Hammersmith. The Sipsmith company had actually wanted to open earlier, but a major stumbling block to this was HM Revenue & Customs, because the quantity of gin they planned to produce at the time – less than 300 litres – was so small it would be technically classified as 'moonshine'.

Thankfully the authorities were eventually persuaded, and now Sipsmith produce a London Dry Gin using the one-shot method. Vodka is also made along with a number of spirit infusions, and one of the highlights of a visit to the distillery is to see its wall of spirited infusions in large, clear containers.

In 2014 the company moved to its current site, close to the Fuller's brewery in West London, and it now has three stills, named Prudence, Patience and Constance! Prudence's bespoke design combines a pot with a carter head and a column still, which makes it incredibly versatile, allowing the company to distil both vodka and gin from the same still – albeit with a cleaning day in between. The swan motif on the Sipsmith trademark is a reference to the 'swan's neck' pipe where the spirit vapour turns above the still.

The botanicals

Sipsmith uses ten carefully selected botanicals from around the globe to make its gin. The skill of the distiller is to get these botanicals to release their essential oils into the spirit. The prime botanical is the juniper berries. Sipsmith macerate the berries in warm spirit overnight to burst the skins and release the essences.

Next come the orange skins. The oranges used are grown along the streets of Seville, Spain, and are also known as 'bitter orange'. This fruit has a wonderful tartness that delivers a zesty citrus note to the palate, with marmalade overtones. The other key citrus element, lemon peel, adds a subtle brightness to the citrus notes.

Next comes orris, the root of the iris flower, which delivers a delicate floral, fragrant note while also binding the other botanicals together to deliver a harmonious flavour profile. Angelica, which is similar to orris root, acts as another binding agent to promote the harmony of the botanicals. It also adds its own dry characteristic and provides a long, dry finish.

Liquorice root adds an attractive bittersweet undertone, and equally importantly neutralises any bitterness from other botanicals to allow their properties to shine. By contrast, Madagascan cinnamon bark – which is similar to and from the same family as cassia – adds a delicately sweet spiciness to the mix. Cassia bark, hailing all the way from China, is also

▼ The heart of a good gin is the depth and character quality of juniper berries.

▼ Seville oranges growing in Southern Spain. Bitter orange adds a zesty, tangy note to any infusion.

▲ Liquorice add a bittersweet undertone to gin, while subduing the bitterness of other ingredients.

▲ Chinese cassia bark contributes notes of sweetness and warmth to the gin.

▼ Shelled almonds bring a hint of spice and marzipan notes to some brands of gin.

present, and adds a hint of sweet and warm spice. Spanish ground almond is used to bring delicate spiciness and marzipan notes and adds depth and body to the gin. Finally, mellow spiciness and a long finish, with hints of citrus and peppery ginger, is derived from the addition of coriander seed.

Making a perfect sloe gin – the Sipsmith way

According to Sipsmith founder Jared Brown, people making sloe gin at home often make two mistakes: they add sugar at the start of the process and use cheap gin. He says: 'Contrary to popular belief, there's very little point in adding sugar at the outset. Saturating the spirit with sugar prevents it from extracting the natural fruit sugars – and other flavours – from the sloes.'

As far as he's concerned you only add sugar at the start if you want to use the sloes for baking or chocolates, not for good sloe gin.

'One of the common complaints about the standard sloe recipes is that some years they produce a too-sweet liqueur, while other years they aren't sweet enough,' says Jared. 'Sweetening to taste at the end of the maceration yields a perfect batch every time. If you use simple syrup instead of granulated sugar you don't have to wait for the crystals to dissolve.'

His recipe for making sugar syrup is very simple. He recommends you should combine equal measures of sugar and water in a saucepan over low heat. 'Warm the mixture until the sugar dissolves, then allow it to cool. If you prefer a higher-strength sloe gin, it's possible to make syrup with three parts sugar and two parts water to reduce dilution.'

He also says that it's best to add the sugar to the macerated sloes sparingly: 'Add just a little syrup at first, as it sometimes requires only a fraction of the quantity called for in the recipe.'

As for using a cheap gin, Jared says: 'Far from masking bad spirit, sloes highlight a gin's quality or lack thereof. It's worth splashing out the price of a high-street cappuccino to upgrade to a better gin. Also, look in the liquor cabinet. If there's a dusty bottle of grappa, brandy or Irish whiskey lying around, these are also great for making sloe liqueurs.'

▼ When making an infusion using gin, Sipsmith recommends macerating the fruit before adding sugar. (Tim Hampson)

▲ The best time to pick sloes is when they are ripe, or they can be bought on the internet.

▼ In Britain, Autumn is usually the time to pick sloes, but if it has been a good summer they can ripen early.

He also recommends adding a crushed almond to the infusion: 'One ingredient that occasionally appeared in 19th century recipes was almonds. A crushed almond, added at the start of the maceration process, highlights the marzipan character of the stone fruit without the added effort of crushing a few sloe stones.'

He says there are some absurd myths about harvesting and processing sloes floating around, and he wants to dispel a few of these. For instance, there's no point in waiting for the first frost to pick sloes, though it's great advice if the frost happens to coincide with the ripening of the sloes. 'Like all fruit,' he says, 'it's best to pick sloes when they're ripe. So just squeeze one. If it feels like a rock, it's not ripe. Ripe sloes yield to the touch like small ripe plums.' He says there's no need to try each one – if a few are ripe, then the entire crop is ready. He adds that if sloes can't be found close to home it's easy to buy them on eBay.

Jared also says that there's no point in pricking the berries before use. 'What you really need to do is place the sloes in a freezer bag and freeze them for a day or two. The point of pricking them is to rupture the fruit, allowing the flavour to leak out while they're sitting in the gin. Freezing ruptures the sloes completely and evenly.'

So, Jared's secret to making the best sloe gin? Find good sloes, on the land or online, freeze them overnight, add enough fruit to almost half-fill a jar and top it up with good-quality gin. Then wait at least three months. Only then should you add sugar or syrup to taste.

'It couldn't be easier, better or simpler – unless, of course, you just buy a bottle of Sipsmith Sloe Gin instead!' But then he would say that, wouldn't he?

LIMONCELLO – THE TASTE OF SOUTHERN ITALY

There's more legend to the story of Limoncello than fact, but that doesn't stop this intensely flavoured drink being a classic which most people have encountered on a trip to Southern Italy, where it's a favourite in many bars. In fact many tourists sip it as a summer refresher, not realising it's made not just with lemons and sugar but also 40% alcohol.

Lemons are thought to have originated in Southern China and were later introduced into Assyria, where they were discovered by soldiers serving under Alexander the Great, who took them back to Greece. From here their cultivation spread around the Mediterranean.

Italy is the world's largest producer of lemons, and lemon trees seem to grow everywhere. In fact it seems that the rougher the ground is, the more the trees thrive, growing large fruits packed with citric acid. It isn't unusual to see people eating them sliced thin, with just a dusting of sugar. Indeed, given the volume and quality of lemons grown in Italy it would be surprising if an alcoholic drink of some kind wasn't made or flavoured with lemons.

Stories abound about limoncello's origins. Some say it was made to be drunk by fishermen as they prepared to sail their boats out into the still, cold night before dawn. Others claim it was made by monks eager to find something they could sell to augment the income their monastery needed to finance its good works. According to one story it was invented in the early 20th century by a Capri guesthouse owner, Maria Antonia Farace, who produced it for her guests.

▲ Limoncello might claim to be an ancient drink, but it was invented in the 20th century.

▼ Lemons now grow widely around the Mediterranean and North Africa, but they originate from China.

However, the truth may be a little more prosaic, since some say the drink was created as recently as 1988, when businessman Massimo Canale patented the trademark Limoncello and began selling his product to local bars and restaurants. Whatever the truth, what started as a local drink is now sold around the world.

It's a perfect sipping liqueur when served chilled in a long, tall, thin glass. It's a perfect partner to Italian sweets such as tiramisu, and many mixologists are now exploring its possibilities for use in cocktails. It has become liquid gold in a bottle.

The intensely flavoured and aromatic drink is made from lemon zest, spirit and sugar. The secret to its success is the unique flavour of the lemons which are grown in Southern Italy, and the intense aroma of the essential oils in the zest.

Although organic lemons from Southern Italy aren't readily available to everyone it's still possible to make limoncello at home, using the zest of unwaxed yellow lemons, vodka and sugar syrup. Simply, all you need to do is steep the zest in vodka for between two and three days. The liquid is then strained and you add sugar syrup to taste. The better the lemons you use, the better the taste. The amount of sugar is really up to you and how sweet you like it. Finally, strain your infusion into decorative bottles and add a few strips of lemon zest to each. The perfect gift to give to friends.

Today many variations of the liqueur are being made and there's no one recipe – though every producer says that theirs is the authentic one. So, try it at home and make your own authentic limoncello.

Making your own limoncello

If all goes well this lemon liqueur could be on a par with anything you can find on Italy's sun-kissed Amalfi coast. If you fancy being adventurous, try using the zest of limes. If making a smaller volume, simply scale back the ingredients.

Ingredients
- 10 lemons
- 750ml vodka
- Approximately a litre of sugar syrup (the amount is up to you – I prefer mine less sweet)

Method
1. Carefully cut the zest off the lemons – avoid using the white pith, which has some off flavours.
2. Slice the peel into thin strips.
3. Put into a container that can be sealed and cover with the vodka. Put into a dark place for a few days.
4. Strain and taste the infusion and add sugar syrup to your taste.
5. Serve very cold. As it contains vodka, it can be chilled in a freezer without freezing.

Whether you try it as an aperitif, a digestif or a cocktail, this liqueur's sweet lemony flavour should be crisp, aromatic and refreshing. Limoncello is also ideal to sip as a long drink – cover the bottom of a tall ice-filled glass with a generous splash of chilled limoncello and top up with soda water, tonic water, cola, cranberry juice, lemonade or other soft drink of your choice.

◀ **Limoncello is a fantastic ingredient for many cocktails. It is a real summer refresher.**

CHARTREUSE – GREEN ELIXIR

Is this really the elixir of life? The roots of many liqueurs are long and come from a time when alchemists were trying to invent potions that would enable them to live forever or cure common ailments. And so it was in the monastery where St Bruno had founded the Carthusian Oder of monks more than 1,000 years ago, at Chartreuse, near Grenoble in the French Alps.

A monastery would have been a good place to develop potions. From the earliest beginnings monks toiled in gardens filled with herbs, spices and vegetables. Places of learning and great knowledge, some in the brotherhood made bread, cheese, beer, wine and distillations. This work continues today within the ancient monastery of Chartreuse deep in the mountains of the same name, where three monks jealously guard the secret of their green treasure.

The recent history of their elixir stretches back more than 500 years, to 1605, when – allegedly – French diplomat and soldier François-Annibal d'Estrées came to the isolated monastery and presented its monks with a battered manuscript, on which was purportedly an elixir that claimed to sustain long life. The monks are said to have then spent 32 years poring over the near indecipherable recipe. During the next century they tinkered with it, tweaked it, improved it, and probably changed it completely, until in 1764 they announced the creation of Green Chartreuse. The credit for having made sense of the original scribbling is ascribed to one Brother Antoine, who is reputed to have created a substance known

▲ **The largest liqueur cellar in the world, storing barrels of Chartreuse, in Grenoble, France.** (Courtesy Getty)

as *Élixir Végétal de la Grande-Chartreuse*. The bright green elixir is said to have been composed of 132 different herbs, flowers and other closely-guarded secret ingredients, which are added to an alcohol base. Some of the extracts were distilled, and it's this which helps create the green colour from the chlorophyll in the verdant plants.

The French Revolution changed everything in 1789. All members of all religious orders were ordered out of the country. Most of the Chartreuse monks left France in 1793. They made a copy of the manuscript, kept by one of them who remained in the monastery; another monk was in charge of the original manuscript. Shortly after leaving Chartreuse he was arrested and sent to prison in Bordeaux. Fortunately, however, he wasn't searched and was able to secretly pass the original manuscript to Dom Basile Nantas, who later sold it to a pharmacist in Grenoble.

The pharmacist, however, never produced the elixir and in 1810, when the Emperor Napoleon ordered all the 'secret' recipes of medicines to be sent to the Ministry of the Interior, the pharmacist dutifully complied with the law. But the manuscript was returned to him, as it was not considered a secret. When he died his heirs sent the manuscript to the monks, who had returned to their monastery in 1816. They were expelled again in 1903 and moved – pew, prayer book and precious recipe – to Tarragona in Spain. However, production of the green liqueur under the name Chartreuse had to stop, as the French Government told them they couldn't use the word unless they made it in France.

Instead, they sold a drink called Tarragone. By 1929 the monks were back on French soil and production of Green Chartreuse had resumed. But luck wasn't with them, and their distillery was destroyed by a mudslide in 1935.

On the move again, the distillery was established in an old warehouse owned by the monks in Voiron, where all Chartreuse is made today. However, the monastery of Chartreuse itself still has a vital role to play in the making of the liqueur, as it is home not just to the original (and still secret) recipe but is also where the botanicals are stored and blended before being transported to nearby Voirin, where they are left to macerate in alcohol before being distilled. Finally, the liqueur is aged for eight years in huge oak casks in the world's longest liqueur maturation cellar.

The best way to drink this green liqueur is very cold with plenty of ice, but if you don't like that try it long with soda or a ginger ale. One variant, Green Chaud, is said to be drunk *après-ski* in the nearby Alps. This consists of a teaspoon of Green Chartreuse in a mug of creamy hot chocolate. A yellow, lighter, smoother version of Chartreuse was produced for the first time in the 1830s.

BENEDICTINE – A TIMELESS CLASSIC

Burnley in Lancashire, in North-West England, probably has many claims to fame. Its football team is one of only three to have won all four divisional titles, along with Wolves and Preston. And in the Second World War it became home to London's Old Vic theatre, which left London to avoid the Blitz. But what is little known is that the town's miners' and working men's clubs were once the world's largest purveyors of Benedictine, a French liqueur made in a monastery in Normandy, and even today more Benedictine liqueur is drunk in East Lancashire – the area that includes Accrington, Blackburn and Burnley – than anywhere else outside France.

The link between Burnley and Benedictine dates to the days following the end of World War One when, from June to October 1919, Z Company of the 11th Battalion of the East Lancashire Regiment – better known locally as the famous 'Accrington Pals' – was based in the Le Havre, Harfleur and Fécamp area, close to the Benedictine Abbey that produces the liqueur.

The 'war to end all wars' had had a terrible effect on the people of Burnley. In this respect it was probably no different than many other places where soldiers were recruited, but over 4,000 men from Burnley were killed in the conflict – about 15% of the male working-age population. Post-war in France the battalion's survivors relaxed in the bars and cafés in and around wherever they were billeted. A particular attraction of the Harfleur area is Le Palais Bénédictine, a huge neo-Gothic building in the town centre, where Benedictine has been produced since 1863, so it's possible that, in 1919, parties of the Pals visited the distillery. What's more certain is that Benedictine was sold in every café and bar in Harfleur and Le Havre, and the Pals got a taste for it.

So it's understandable that on finally returning home the former combatants were convinced that a glass of 'Bene'

◄ **The story of Benedictine is told in stained glass windows at the monastery.** (Courtesy Benedictine)

▶ **Soldiers from Lancashire got a taste for Benedictine while serving in France.** (Courtesy Benedictine)

▶ **It is not just Benedictine in barrels that is kept under lock and key, the recipe is too.** (Courtesy Benedictine)

would raise their spirits and improve their health. Consequently such was the demand for the drink that sales in East Lancashire soon amounted to most of the total sales in Britain, and so it has continued to this day.

The makers of Benedictine say that it's best drunk over ice after at the end of a meal. However, the former Pals had their own variation. They drank it hot, as a toddy mixed with boiling water, and this version of the drink is still sold at the town football club on match days – fans says there's no better way of keeping the cold out.

Benedictine is made using 27 different plants and spices, each of which is absolutely vital to the final recipe. Like many liqueurs, the recipe for making Benedictine is known only to its master blender, but the three key ingredients are angelica, with its balsamic and warming aroma; hyssop, which has a strong and slightly bitter flavour; and lemon balm, for its tangy, aromatic, lemon essences. Serious home infusers should try making their own infusion using these ingredients.

Other ingredients in the drink include vanilla from Madagascar and myrrh from Saudi Arabia, as well as nutmeg, mace, cloves, cinnamon, cardamom and saffron. Indeed, the colonisation of the world by European countries was often in search not only of gold but also of equally valuable spices.

The 27 ingredients of Benedictine are carefully weighed and sorted. Vanilla and lemon zest are macerated in a mixture of water and alcohol for up to six months. The carefully weighed ingredients are then separated into four different preparations. The first is the macerated vanilla and lemon, the second is double distilled in a pot still, the third undergoes a single distillation and the fourth goes through a double distillation process.

Each 'alcoholate', as they're known to the monks, is placed separately into its own large oak cask for three months. The rich oak maturation gives each of the liquids flavour and colour. The next stage is to blend the four barrels into a larger oak barrel, where it will stay for a further 12 months. After eight months, honey, caramel and saffron are added. These add colour and depth of flavour to the liqueur. From beginning to end the process has taken more than two years. The result is a complex canvas of citrus, herbs and spices.

In France Benedictine is usually drunk as a digestif. (A good meal will begin with an aperitif, but the digestif is consumed at the end of a meal, and is believed to aid the digestion.) It's sweet but not overpowering and, as the former 'Accrington Pals' discovered on cold winter nights in Lancashire, it's long and marvellously warming.

Benedictine is today one of the world's greatest herbal liqueurs, still made to a recipe dating from 1510 that was developed by Venetian monk Don Bernardo Vincellia. It's come a long way since it was developed to combat malaria!

SOUTHERN COMFORT – NONE GENUINE BUT MINE

Southern Comfort is America's greatest contribution to the world of liqueurs. South Comfort, or Cuff and Buttons, as it was once called, can trace its history back to 1874. The original recipe was created by Martin Wilkes Heron, a bar tender in New Orleans, who wanted to make American whisky – or whiskey, as they prefer to spell it – more palatable.

(Courtesy Southern Comfort)

Unrefined whisky is a harsh drink. To make it the distillers first make something similar to a strong beer. The chosen grain – often barley is used – is fermented to about 8% in strength. However, unlike beer, which is also made from fermented grain, hops aren't added, and it doesn't matter what the liquid – or 'wash', as it's called in a distillery – looks, smells or tastes like.

The wash will then be distilled, which involves heating it until the alcohol starts to boil and steam is created. The water, which has a higher boiling point, is left behind, while the steam, which contains the alcohol, is collected and cooled. This cooled steam forms a clear, colourless liquid that's high in alcohol – it could be 80% ABV, though in the case of some highly efficient stills the alcohol content could be even higher.

This clear, strong spirit is sometimes called 'moonshine'. To transform it into whisky it has to be put into an oak barrel. All the colour and taste of the whisky comes from the wooden barrel in which the spirit is stored. In the US the spirit has to be stored in a barrel for at least two years before it can be called whisky. In the UK it has to be stored for a minimum of three years. Even at two or three years old, whisky can still be a callow, rough drink.

Southern Comfort's Irish-born inventor, Martin Heron, had travelled along the length of the mighty Mississippi River before, some time in the early 1870s, he took a job as a barman and rectifier in a bar in the thriving port city of New Orleans. After tasting and serving the spirits in this bar he decided his customers needed a smoother, better-tasting whisky. So, in order to improve the harsh, unrefined barrelled whisky available at the time, he began adding various spirits, spices and flavours.

After much experimentation he hit upon a combination of flavours that resulted in a remarkably smooth, refreshing and easy to drink alternative to the rough spirits he normally served. He called his creation Cuffs and Buttons (a rival bar

sold a drink called Hats and Tails), and it was a big hit with his customers, especially the women.

In 1885 the city hosted the New Orleans Exposition, a celebration of the brave, energetic world of burgeoning American commerce, and Heron decided that his Cuffs and Buttons needed a name and image that reflected the energy of the American south. Thus was born the name we use today – Southern Comfort.

In 1889 Heron moved to Memphis Tennessee, where he achieved a lifelong dream of owning his own bar. His creation Southern Comfort sold well. He then made the decision to bottle his drink. He registered its name as a trademark and began putting on the bottles' labels 'M.W. Heron's Famous Southern Comfort: None Genuine But Mine'. In the early 1900s he moved to St Louis, Missouri, taking the production of his drink with him.

The original Southern Comfort was a spirit blended with a wide range of fruits and herbs, possibly including peaches, oranges, lemons, apricots, vanilla and cinnamon, which was matured in oak barrels. The drink is sweet, fruity and strong, which makes it great for making cocktails. In 1939 the Scarlett O'Hara cocktail was invented as a tribute to the famous movie *Gone with the Wind*. It is mixed with Southern Comfort, cranberry juice and fresh lime.

Over time the drink's feminine image has acquired a rock and roll aura. In the 1960s, for instance, singer Janis Joplin would often appear on stage with a bottle.

DRAMBUIE – THE DRINK THAT SATISFIES

Most liqueurs have a neutral grain spirit as their base, to which fruit, herbs, spices and sugar are added. Not so with Drambuie, which has blended whisky as its base. But like many liqueurs the origin of Drambuie is shrouded in myth and mystery and, like many tales from Scotland, it involves Bonnie Prince Charlie.

The story begins in July 1746, when Prince Charles Edward Stuart, the Bonnie Prince, was fleeing after his traumatic defeat by the English at the Battle of Culloden. This battle was the last of the great Jacobite risings – popular attempts to reinstate a Stuart monarch on the throne of Britain – and ended Charlie's dream of restoring the Stuarts to the throne. He was pursued by the victorious Duke of Cumberland's troops across the Highlands and Islands of Western Scotland, and during his flight many loyal Jacobites offered Charles shelter from his pursuers. One such supporter was clan leader John MacKinnon, who helped the Prince escape from the Isle of Skye.

As thanks for his help, the Prince is said to have rummaged through his luggage and handed MacKinnon the recipe for his favourite drink, an extraordinary elixir that would, many years later, become known to the world as Drambuie. It does seem fanciful, to say the least, that an escaping Prince, fearful for his life as pursuing troops got nearer, would seek out a piece

▼ The Scarlett O'Hara cocktail was invented as an alcoholic tribute to the classic 1930s film *Gone with the Wind*.

Cath Harries

of paper with a secret recipe written on it and pass it on to Mackinnon, but such is the tale.

However, it is certainly likely that a fiery spirit was being made in Scotland at the time, which went on to be known as whiskey. To make this spirit palatable it seems equally probable that it would have been flavoured with herbs and spices and used for medicinal purposes. Its strong flavours are also likely to have been softened and made more palatable by the honey that was produced by bees feeding on moorland heather, together with other herbs and spices.

The story would have it that, more than 130 years later, Charles Stuart's recipe came into the hands of John Ross, who ran the Broadford Hotel on Skye and in 1873 started to make the liqueur to serve to his customers. The delighted drinkers are said to have remarked in Gaelic that it was, '*An dram buidheach*,' the drink that satisfies. The phrase became shortened to Drambuie.

The name stuck, and in 1893 John's son James registered it as a trademark. When one Malcolm MacKinnon travelled from Skye to Edinburgh in 1900 to work in the wines and spirits business, he saw the commercial opportunities for the liqueur, and in 1909 started to produce it on the Scottish mainland. By 1914 he had established the Drambuie Liqueur Company.

The drink quickly caught on. It was on sale in the House of Lords in 1916, and a year later Buckingham Palace bought 12 bottles of Drambuie. It also started to sell well in America, and managed to survive Prohibition by being sold illegally in speakeasies, where its sweet, honey tones would be used to

mask the harsh tones of the illegally-made moonshine with which it was mixed.

Today Drambuie is a component of one of the world's classic cocktails, the Rusty Nail, which became a favourite with singers such as the legendary Frank Sinatra, a member of the 'Rat Pack', which also included Dean Martin and Sammy Davis Junior. It's probable that it was a refinement of the drinks sold in the illegal speakeasies of East Coast America.

The creation of the Rusty Nail recipe is usually attributed to Manhattan's 21 Club, and its name caught on when it was endorsed by the then chairwoman of the Drambuie Liqueur Company, Gina MacKinnon. It quickly became the must-make drink in many middle-class American households, eager to show off their wealth and sophistication.

To make Drambuie, first you must have a good malt whisky base. You need a blend of grain whisky and a selection of the finest Speyside and Highland malts – some malts are aged up to 15 years, adding real depth to the whisky base. To this is added the special blend of herbs and spices and, of course, honey.

Cath Harries

BAILEYS IRISH CREAM – HERE'S TO US

Unlike many other successful liqueurs Baileys doesn't have a long history shrouded in mystery. There are no stories of someone discovering the dusty notebook of a long dead alchemist seeking the elixir of life. Instead, it's a triumph of modern technology and marketing, and is now probably the biggest-selling liqueur brand in the world.

The idea for the drink was conceived in 1970, when David Dand, who was then the managing director of Gilbeys of Ireland, spotted the opportunity for a new drink brand and seized on it. It was launched in 1974, by a team who wanted to market a drink that appealed to women at a time when many spirits, particularly whiskies, were targeted at male consumers. Another motivation was the company's overproduction of Irish whiskey – they had more than they could sell. The resulting liqueur successfully married whiskey, hot coffee, cream and sugar.

Irish whiskey mixed with cream was a common home remedy for people with a stomach upset. It was also very easy to make. Whiskey and cream were just mixed together. However, the transition from a simple home remedy to a commercial product isn't always easy. The main problem was that the two elements would only remain mixed together for a short time and quickly separated. In addition the cream could curdle. It took three years of product development to get the two to live together comfortably, by the addition of a little chocolate, sugar and vanilla in one homogenised drink. The trick they developed was the ability to homogenise alcohol, some whiskey and cream with a little vegetable oil. This prevents the alcohol and cream from getting separated during the process.

The team of drinks boffins charged with developing Baileys, led by Steve Wilson, was astonished by the success of their drink, which has gone on to be much mimicked by other companies. 'We kept building bigger factories but it still took us five years for production to keep up with demand,' says Steve.

So where does the name come from – was there ever a Mr Bailey? Was he the inventor of the drink, or a famous Irishman whose name deserves to be celebrated? Sadly, no, the truth is far more prosaic. The drink name is entirely fictional and was inspired by the name of a hotel in London. According to one account the name is Irish without being clichéd, and was thought up by a drinks industry executive who was staring out of his office window at the Bailey hotel.

The Celtic motifs on the label might indicate an ancient past, even the signature of R.A. Bailey seems to indicate a long history, but they're just window dressing. However, the milk does come from 40,000 Irish cows, the whiskey is

◀▼ **Despite the drink's name, there is no Mr Bailey. Its inspiration was a hotel sign in London. A glass of Baileys is the drink of choice at many Christmas celebrations.**

Irish, and the drink is made in Ireland. But much more than a triumph of marketing Baileys is also an enjoyable drink, and its makers have since gone on to introduce hazelnut, coffee, mint and caramel versions amongst others.

Now owned by the international spirits giant Diageo, Baileys recently released the advertising campaign 'Here's to us', which is female-centric and designed to introduce a new generation of Millennial women to the brand. However – and thankfully for male fans of the drink – they also recognise that many men like to enjoy a glass of Baileys on the rocks.

Irish cream

Have a go at making your own Irish cream.

Ingredients
- 250ml single cream
- 400g can condensed milk
- 250ml single cream
- 350ml Irish whiskey
- 1 tsp coffee essence or instant coffee
- 1 tsp chocolate extract
- 1 tsp vanilla extract
- 1 tsp almond extract (optional)

Method
1 Put all the ingredients in a blender and whiz for 30 seconds.
2 Pour into a clean container and keep in the fridge.

ADVOCAAT – OVEREGGING THE SPIRIT

Two generations ago the Christmas drink for women of a certain age was a snowball. Yellow in colour and with a custard-like consistency, it was a mixture of advocaat and lemonade.

What might have been seen as a fad of the 1970s was in fact a drink that has a history going back more than 400 years. Advocaat is a rich, smooth cream liqueur created from egg yolks, sugar, brandy and vanilla. Like many drinks, its early history is obscure. It was either derived from a popular, boozy medieval drink called a posset, or a mushy mix made by Dutch colonists from the fruit of avocado pears in South America.

According to Bols, the makers of one of the best-known brands of advocaat, its origins go back to a time when the

▼ Irish cream is easy to make and has a touch of luxury, especially when served with Christmas home baking.

Netherlands was at the centre of world trade. The Bols family started distilling liqueurs in Amsterdam in 1575. The first flavours were cumin, cardamom and orange, as Dutch boats sailed the world collecting herbs and spices, many of which were used as flavourings in alcoholic drinks.

Advocaat, say Bols, originates from Surinam in South America, the Dutch colonists of which were credited with making an alcoholic drink using the avocado pears that grew there. The soft, oily flesh of these pears would be mushed up and mixed with rum or other locally available spirit. The Dutch then took the avocado pears to Indonesia, where they were planted so that colonists could continue to enjoy their pear and spirit drink. Dutch traders returning home, however, found that avocados wouldn't grow in the temperate climate of Europe, so they devised instead a drink using egg yolks and alcohol.

The recipe is essentially an eggnog, a stirred custard – a mixture of cream or milk, egg and alcohol. Food historians say that the modern eggnog is descended from a thick, late-medieval concoction called a posset that included hot milk, eggs and alcohol enhanced by honey and whatever spices were to hand.

Some traditional advocaat recipes recommend serving it in a tall glass topped with whipped cream, and served with a sprinkling of cocoa powder over the top. This would probably need to be eaten with a spoon rather than sipped. Egg-based drinks also found popularity in the new American colonies, where nearly everyone had access to cows, chickens and rum.

One English recipe from 1671 describes making a posset using cream, cinnamon, mace, 18 egg yolks and some egg whites to which strong fortified wine is added. It doesn't sound that different from a recipe for advocaat.

Several Dutch companies still make advocaat, including De Kuyper and Cooyman's. Versions are also made in the US, Australia, Belgium, Germany and Poland.

Making your own advocaat

Ingredients
- 10 egg yolks
- 200g caster sugar
- 1 vanilla pod
- 350ml brandy
- 1 tsp vanilla extract
- cinnamon, to serve

Method
1 Cut the vanilla pod in half lengthways and with a sharp knife scrape the seeds out and place in a heatproof bowl. Add the egg yolks and sugar to the bowl and whisk until the mixture is pale and thick. Continue whisking, while slowly pouring in the brandy.
2 Place the bowl over a pan of simmering water and heat, stirring continuously, until it thickens to a custard-like consistency. Be careful not to overheat the mixture, as you don't want it to boil. Stir in the vanilla extract.
3 Pour into a container and chill in the fridge. Serve in small glasses with a sprinkle of cinnamon on top.

To make a snowball cocktail, mix one part of the advocaat (100ml) with two parts of lemonade (200ml), pour into a large wine glass and, for a touch of 1970s sophistication, top with a glacé cherry on a stick. Another variant is the Bombardino, a winter favourite in the Italian Alps. Brandy and advocaat are mixed in equal proportions, heated, and then topped with whipped cream. It's a drink for *aprés-ski* rather than before.

CHERRY BRANDY – SWEET CLASS IN A GLASS

According to the original recipe the cherry liqueur came from the Danish company Heering. Today cherry brandy is one of the most popular liqueurs in the world, and is made by macerating cherries in a pure spirit. Sometimes the spirit is grape-based, but a grain-based vodka can be used too. Technically it's a liqueur, as the fruit flavours the spirit, whereas a true brandy would be distilled from the fruit itself. One of the most famous cocktails in the world, Singapore Sling, was created around 1915 in the Raffles hotel in Singapore by cocktail genius Ngiam Tong Boon. The drink gets its distinctive pink hue from the use of cherry liqueur.

The Heering company was set up in 1818 in Copenhagen by grocer Peter Heering. His variant of cherry liqueur is made using whole Danish cherries of the Sven variety, which are lightly crushed, stones and all. The cherries are then macerated together with spices and alcohol for at least three years in oak barrels. It is the cherry stones that give the drink its distinctive almond twang. It's a deep, brick red colour and has an intense aroma of cherries, almond and some herbal notes. And just like a Singapore Slim, the finish is long, warm and sweet.

Another well-known cherry liqueur comes from the Dutch company De Kuyper, founded in 1695 by barrel maker Petrus de Kuyper. His third son Jan opened a distillery in Schiedam and a generation later the company opened its Rotterdam distillery. Its cherry brandy is made using small, dark, ripe but bitter Marasca cherries, which are sliced and macerated in pure neutral spirit and then subtly enhanced with spices including cinnamon and cloves before being blended with some brandy.

To macerate the cherries, Heering's distillers fill one of the underground tanks in the distillery with a mixture of water and alcohol (between 35% and 80% ABV). Once the tank is filled to the right level the ingredients are put into sacks and lowered on ropes into the liquid, where they're left to steep for ten days to six weeks. The fine essential oils are rapidly absorbed into the solution, but insoluble substances take longer. It's down to the skill of the distiller to decide how long the ingredients should remain suspended in the solution.

Cherries were introduced into Britain by the Romans in about 1 AD, and legend has it that cherry trees can be found alongside the routes marched by Roman soldiers. Once we had thousands of acres of cherry orchards, but over the last century Britain has lost 90% of these. However, the fruit is undergoing something of a renaissance at the moment and new trees are being planted – which is good news, since there can be few things better to make than your own cherry liqueur.

▶ **Cherry brandy is one of the world's most popular infusions.**
(Courtesy Heering)

Cherry Liqueur

Ingredients
- 900g cherries, fresh or frozen
- 150g white sugar
- 300ml vodka, or a mixture of vodka and brandy
- 1 stick of cinnamon (optional)
- Sugar syrup, to taste (optional)

Method
1 Put the cherries into a large Kilner jar and add the sugar. Seal with the lid and shake vigorously, then add the vodka or brandy and cinnamon, if using.
2 Leave the sealed container in a dark place for at least six weeks, shaking every few days.
3 Strain thoroughly and taste, adding sugar syrup if needed, before bottling.

Cath Harries

APPEALING ORANGES– SPIRITS WITH ZEST

Some of the best liqueurs in the world are made from the aromatic and flavoursome skins of inedible orange citrus fruits. The dried fragrant peel is steeped in a still with alcohol and water. After soaking for several days the peel is removed and other spices might be added. The resultant spirit will have a citrus flavour – fruity, with varying degrees of bitterness. It is naturally colourless, but colouring is often added, most commonly blue or orange, which brings an exotic, vibrant colour to many cocktails.

Many of these drinks are made with dried peel of bitter oranges grown on the Caribbean island of Curaçao. The peel comes from the laraha citrus fruit, a variation of the sweet Valencia orange originally planted on the island by Spanish colonists in the first part of the 16th century. The poor soil on Curaçao resulted in small, bitter fruits that proved to be almost inedible, but the flavourful skins were ideal for adding flavour to spirits.

The island's name is now applied to a number of liqueurs made using fruit grown elsewhere in the world.

Liqueurs of this style are often classified by the generic names of curaçao or triple sec. Broadly speaking, curaçaos draw on the Dutch tradition of liqueur making. The Dutch were some of the world's greatest traders in the 16th century and had soon mastered the art and skill of distilling, often preserving in spirits the spices, herbs and fruits they brought home.

Triple sec, a term used for many orange-flavoured liqueurs, draws instead on French heritage. The derivation of the term isn't clear, though some believe that the 'triple' prefix refers to the number of times the alcohol is distilled; others says it describes the intensity of the orange flavour. 'Sec' could mean dry, meaning that it's less sweetened than Dutch liqueurs.

Cath Harries

Senior Liqueur

Senior Liqueur

Cath Harries

Today triple secs are usually clear and made with a neutral spirit, whereas curaçaos may start that way but are coloured blue, red, yellow or orange. French Cointreau is probably the most recognised brand of orange liqueur in the triple sec style, while Grand Marnier, which is also French, is more in line with the Dutch curaçao style, as it has an aged brandy base.

Made with the peel of bitter and sweet oranges, Cointreau has been a worldwide legend since its creation in 1849. It combines four ingredients – alcohol, water, sugar and orange peel. The peel doesn't all come from the island of Curaçao but might be sourced from many other countries, including Brazil, Spain and Ghana. Most of the peel is dried, but some fresh, sweet Spanish orange peels are macerated in alcohol, giving candied vanilla notes. The bitter orange peel provides fresh, zesty aromas to the drink.

Grand Marnier, which is marketed as Cordon Rouge, was created in 1880 by Alexandre Marnier-Lapostolle. Made from a blend of cognac brandy, distilled essence of bitter orange and sugar, it is drunk neat as an aperitif and is also used in many cocktails.

There are many other variations on the citrus theme. Mandarine Napoleon uses mandarins steeped in ten-year-old cognac. To this are added a number of botanicals including nutmeg, cinnamon, cloves, cardamom, angelica, green tea and black tea.

De Kuyper's Triple Sec is an example of a clear liqueur that has intense orange flavours that are a mixture of sweet and bitter.

Orange liqueur

Making a triple sec-style drink at home is easy, and it is fun experimenting with a variety of citrus fruits in addition to oranges – tangerines, mandarins, lemons, limes and grapefruit, or a mixture of them, can all be used. It's also fun trying brandy as your base instead of vodka.

▲ The Cosmopolitan cocktail, made from vodka, triple sec, cranberry juice, and freshly squeezed lime juice.

Ingredients
■ 1–2 oranges, unwaxed
■ 350ml vodka or brandy
■ Sugar syrup, to taste (optional)

Method
1 Put the clean zest in the bottom of your sealable jar or container. The bigger your container, the more fruit you should use.
2 Fill with the spirit and leave for no more than a week in a dark cupboard.
3 Occasionally shake the container.
4 Strain well, then taste, adding sugar syrup to taste if needed.

NUTTY KINDS OF DRINK

Nuts such as almonds, hazelnuts and even coconuts provide a bittersweet elegance to many liqueurs. Probably one of the most revered of the nutty style is almond-based amaretto, the Italian name of which means 'a little bitter'. The best examples of amaretto come from Saronno, to the north-west of Milan. When drinking this expect swathes of intense marzipan flavours and Battenberg cake. Rich and fulsome, amaretto is surprisingly well balanced, some people like to add a splash to a cup of hot chocolate or coffee, and it is also used extensively in baking and desserts.

The origins of amaretto are said to go back as far as the Italian Renaissance, and begin with a love story. Legend has it that in 1525 the artist Bernardino Luini, a pupil of Leonardo da Vinci, was commissioned to paint a fresco of the Madonna of the Miracles in Saronno. He chose the beautiful widow of a local innkeeper to inspire his portrayal of the Madonna, and while he was painting her he fell in love. His love was unrequited, as the widow was still in mourning for her deceased husband, but as a gift to show her gratitude and affection she steeped apricot kernels in brandy and presented the resulting amber liquid to Luini.

Today, the best amaretto is usually made using apricot pits, and may also contain almonds, other spices and flavourings. There are several brands available, the two best-known being Luxardo and Disaronno.

Another nutty favourite is Frangelico, which is made with Piedmont hazel nuts. The nuts are shelled, toasted and roasted before infusion in alcohol and water. This mixture is distilled and blended with extracts and distillates from cocoa seeds, vanilla berries and other flavourings, and the concentrate is then blended with a neutral spirit, sugar and water to achieve the required bottling strength. Finally it's left to mature in large vats for six to eight weeks to allow the ingredients to marry together and mellow.

According to legend Frangelico's origin dates back 300 years to a time when monks lived in the hills above Piedmont, one of whom, Fra Angelico, is credited with developing the drink. Another drink with a nut flavour is Malibu, which comprises a blend of light white rum, coconut milk and herbs.

Making a quick and easy amaretto

A speedy amaretto can be made with almond extract.

Ingredients
- 250ml water
- 200g sugar
- 100g demerara sugar
- 350ml vodka
- 50ml natural almond extract
- 2 tsp natural vanilla extract

Method
1 Bring the water to the boil in a saucepan and add in both types of sugar.
2 Turn off the heat and stir well until the sugars have dissolved.
3 Let the sugar syrup cool, add the vodka and the almond and vanilla extract, and stir.
4 Transfer to a bottle. Once cooled it is ready to drink.

Hazelnut liqueur

This recipe can be adapted to make an amaretto, just substitute almonds for the hazelnuts.

Ingredients
- 230g raw hazelnuts, roughly chopped
- 250ml vodka
- 125ml brandy
- 125ml sugar syrup
- 1 vanilla pod

Method
1 Put the hazelnuts, vodka and brandy in a sealable jar, shake, and leave to steep in a dark place at room temperature for two weeks.
2 Add in the sugar syrup to taste, you may need less than 125g. and steep for a few more days.
3 Cut the vanilla pod in half lengthways and scrape out the seeds, add these to the jar and leave for a few more days.
4 Strain well, you may also need to filter through a cheesecloth-lined sieve or paper filter, and then transfer to a bottle.

Making a coconut-flavoured rum

Ingredients
- 1 coconut or a bag of dried shredded coconut
- 750ml white rum
- 300–400ml sugar syrup
- 1 vanilla pod (optional)

Method
1 Break open the coconut, remove its flesh and break into chunks. Shred it in a food processor or use a grater, and transfer to a container
2 Pour the rum over the shredded coconut and leave in a cool dark place for a week. Add the sugar syrup together with the scraped seeds from the vanilla pod, if using, and leave the rum for a few more days, possibly a week.
3 Once you're happy with the flavour, strain and bottle.

COFFEE HAS BEAN – A REAL RUM DRINK

Coffee has come a long way since it was first discovered by Ethiopian nomads in the 11th century, when the wandering goat herders observed that goats which ate the fruit and leaves from one particular type of bush became hyperactive and stayed awake all night. Since then coffee has garnered many more fanciful tales. And, of course, like many other plants that humans started to use it for medicinal purposes, they eventually added alcohol.

Today the two best-known coffee liqueurs in the world are Kahlúa and Tia Maria. Kahlúa claims Mexican heritage, while Tia Maria comes originally from Jamaica and is flavoured with Blue Mountain coffee. Both are relatively low in alcohol, with about 20–25% ABV.

Kahlúa is a blend of Arabica coffee beans, spices, alcohol spirit, sugar syrup and rum. Its story begins in 1936, when four men decided to produce a rum and coffee-based liqueur. One had the idea, two had the money to invest in the project and the fourth was a chemist who knew how to make things

happen. The current owners' delight in telling people that 'there's still a touch of mystery surrounding Kahlúa's exact origins'. Indeed, there is, as according to some the name Kahlúa is derived from the word *kahwa*, which is Arabic slang for coffee. Another version of the Kahlúa story claims its name comes from the Acolhuas, a sister culture of the Aztecs, who arrived in Mexico in 1200.

The manufacturing of Kahlúa is a complicated process. The coffee beans are dried, de-husked and aged for six months, at which point they're roasted, ground up and brewed. Molasses is meanwhile made from sugar cane juice to which water and yeast are added to ferment the mixture, which is then distilled. Afterwards the cane spirit is combined with the brewed coffee extract plus caramel and vanilla. After resting for eight weeks it is filtered, bottled and finally ready for consumption.

Tia Maria is an even newer drink, having been launched in the 1950s using a formula devised by Dr Kenneth Leigh Evans. It was made using Jamaican coffee beans harvested from the foothills of Jamaica's Blue Mountains. Add in citric acid, vanilla, cane spirit then some liquid syrup and you have a concentrate that can be sent around the world for processing and bottling.

However, there's one version of the company's history that is far more romantic. This version has it that Tia Maria dates back to the mid-17th century, when a beautiful young Spanish aristocrat called Tia Maria fled the turmoil of war and emigrated to the island of Jamaica. Her maid saved one family treasure, a small jewellery box containing black pearl earrings and an ancient manuscript with the recipe for a mysterious liqueur. Two centuries later Dr Evans discovered the manuscript with the recipe, and, as they say, the rest is history.

Putting aside the hyperbole, coffee liqueurs are fantastic ingredients for mixologists and chefs. Coffee liqueur provides the foundation for some great cocktails, including Black Russian, White Russian, Mudslide and the Brown Cow.

Homemade coffee liqueur

Ingredients
■ Coarsely ground coffee beans
■ Spirit of your choice – vodka, rum or a mixture of the two
■ Sugar syrup

Method
1 Fill your container to about one third with the ground beans.
2 Fill the container with the spirit.
3 Infuse for 12–24 hours.
4 Strain well.
5 Add sugar syrup to taste. A dark sugar syrup can add complexity to the final drink.

Variants include making the liqueur using made coffee or cold brewed coffee. Steep the ground beans for 12 hours or so. A cold brewed coffee base is slightly less bitter than if the coffee has been mashed hot.

▲ Wormwood is one of the major ingredients in absinthe, a fashionable drink in the nineteenth century.

▲ Green fairy, or La Fee Verte, was the affectionate French nickname given to the celebrated absinthe drink in the nineteenth century.

ABSINTHE –
A BOHEMIAN RHAPSODY

In the mysterious world of spirits, absinthe is one of the most enigmatic. Medicinal elixirs using wormwood are known to have been used by the Egyptians thousands of years ago, and an historical absinthe was probably the predecessor of many of today's anise-based drinks. However, Pierre Ordinaire – a French doctor living in Switzerland – is credited with creating the highly alcoholic present-day elixir absinthe in 1798.

Absinthe is a mixture of liquorice, wormwood bark and other herbs, its name being derived from the scientific name of wormwood, *Artemisia absinthium*. Although sometimes colourless, the slightly bitter spirit is traditionally bright green, which inspired its nickname, *le fee vert*, 'the green fairy'. It became popular in France in the second half of the 19th century following the return home of troops to whom it had been given as a medicine for warding off malaria. Wide-scale mass consumption in place of wine was triggered when in the late 19th century nearly half of France's vines and vineyards were destroyed by the outbreak of the 'phylloxera plague', tiny bugs that attacked the roots of the vines.

The green liqueur was easy to make using industrial alcohol, was flavourful, and was a lot stronger than a glass of wine. It was popularised by famous artists and writers, including Oscar Wilde, Henri de Toulouse-Lautrec, Paul Gaugin, Paul Cézanne, Charles Baudelaire, Edgar Allen Poe and Ernest Hemingway. By the end of the 19th century absinthe had become the spirit of choice, particularly amongst bohemians and artists in Paris, where cocktail hour became known as *l'heure verte*, 'the green hour'.

Absinthe is the base for many cocktails, Hemingway's favourite tipple was said to be Death in the Afternoon, a fusion of champagne and absinthe. Most absinthe drinkers enjoy it served traditionally with an ice-water glass fountain, in which the water drips slowly into the absinthe and creates

the perfect louche, which is the magical opalescent effect that occurs when water mixes with the green fairy.

Another way to serve it is to put a shot into a glass. A slotted spoon shaped like a wormwood leaf is laid flat across the top. A sugar cube is then placed on the spoon – to take away the bitterness of the wormwood in the absinthe – and ice-cold water is slowly added to the sugar. The sugar gradually dissolves and its solution falls into the absinthe.

Over time the drink became associated with public outcry against alcoholism, sometimes called 'absinthism', and there were concerns over its potential effects on the nervous system. This was because wormwood contains the mild

▼ Some bartenders drip water from an ice water fountain through sugar into absinthe.

hallucinogen thujone, which was believed to alter people's behaviour. Indeed, several murderers placed the blame for their behaviour on the drinking of absinthe. Consequently consumption of absinthe was banned in several European countries, including Switzerland and France.

Wormwood was probably blamed wrongly for this wave of unacceptable behaviour, however, since thujone is also found in other herbs, including sage and tarragon. More likely the many reports of strange behaviour following the consumption of absinthe can be more accurately explained by the amount of strong spirit people were drinking and the addition of chemicals put into the drink at the time to make it green or enhance its white, milky cloudiness when water is added.

To make absinthe commercially the herbs and botanicals are infused or macerated in a high proof neutral spirit in an alembic still that's either gently warmed or isn't heated at all. The mixture is then distilled, which effectively separates the volatile oils in the plants and the alcohol, leaving the water behind. Then it's likely that even more herbs are added, such as hyssop and angelica. This adds more flavour to the drink and gives it its green colour.

Make your own absinthe

Making absinthe at home isn't easy, there being so many potential herbs and spices that could be used. However, here is my take using 250ml or so of vodka. I think I'd best describe it as a work in progress.

Ingredients
- 3g wormwood leaves
- 1 star anise, crushed
- 20g fennel leaves, muddled
- 20g angelica stems
- 1 tsp coriander seeds, crushed
- 1 tsp mint leaves, muddled
- Sugar syrup, to taste

Method
1. Other than the sugar syrup, put all the ingredients in a container and cover with the vodka.
2. Leave for two or three weeks and strain well.
3. Add sugar syrup to taste.

LIQUID HEAVEN – CHOCOLATE IN A GLASS

Everyone loves chocolate, don't they? Sweet or bitter, there's probably a style of chocolate for everyone. Today, chocolate is one of the world's favourite comfort foods, but to the ancient Mayans it offered a lot more than comfort – it was considered a powerful aphrodisiac.

The Mayans of Central America are believed to have been the first to discover cocoa, as early as 900 AD. They learned that the beans inside the cocoa pods could be harvested

and made into a liquid that would become a nutritious drink. Mayan chocolate was very different to the chocolate we know today. It was a liquid made from crushed cocoa beans, chilli peppers and water that was poured repeatedly from one cup to another until a frothy foam appeared on top. The word chocolate is said to come from the Mayan word *xocolatl*, which means 'bitter water'.

The French are claimed to have made the first chocolate liqueur towards the end of the 17th century. Most of the earlier versions would have been a blend of a base spirit and dark, bitter chocolate. Spirit and chocolate constitute a harmonious marriage of tastes.

So, having been to a whisky and chocolate tasting I was looking forward to seeing if I could make my own chocolate whisky liqueur. They're a natural combination, as a well-chosen piece of chocolate adds to and draws out flavours from the whisky. The alcohol in the whisky helps break down the flavours in the chocolate, adding to the depth of flavours perceived. The effect is similar to adding a little water to whisky, which similarly opens up the flavours.

Godiva is probably the best-known chocolate liqueur. The chocolate-making company itself was established in 1926, and added a liqueur to its range of products in 1993. The original Godiva liqueur was made with dark chocolate, which was then blended with a base spirit. The company now makes various chocolate variants including white and cappuccino.

To make a smaller or larger batch, just scale the ingredients to suit. Many thanks to Imperial Sugar for the recipe. **bartenders**

Making a chocolate liqueur

Ingredients
- 2 vanilla pods
- 225g granulated sugar
- 120ml water
- 200ml cream
- Pinch of salt
- 90g cocoa powder (the best quality you can find)
- 90g semi-sweet chocolate (chopped fine)
- 1 litre vodka

Method
1 Combine the sugar, water and salt in a pan over a medium heat.
2 Stir until it boils and then let it continue boiling unstirred until the colour becomes deep amber and it smells like caramel, being careful not to let it burn.
3 Remove from the heat and add the cocoa powder half at a time, stirring briskly until everything has combined thoroughly.
4 Add the chocolate and continue stirring until smooth.
5 Pour into a clean glass container, add the vanilla pods and vodka and seal.
6 Shake the container then store in cool dark place. Shake it again every few days for a fortnight.
7 After three or four weeks, strain, bottle and store in a fridge.

White chocolate liqueur

Ingredients
- 250g white chocolate, chopped
- 500ml milk
- 500ml single cream
- 300ml condensed milk
- 150ml vodka, or spirit of your choice
- Vanilla pod, split (optional)

Method
1 Put the chocolate and milk in a saucepan and heat gently until the chocolate has melted.
2 Add the cream, condensed milk and split vanilla pod, if using. Constantly stirring, keep over a low heat until the ingredients are well mixed, no more than ten minutes. Be careful not to let the mixture boil, as the cream will curdle.
3 Let the mixture cool and then chill very well in fridge.
4 Add the alcohol and mix well.
5 Strain and bottle. Store in a fridge for a couple of days before serving.

Mars Bar liqueur

For those with a particularly sweet and decadent tooth, this chocolate caramel liqueur is a bit of fun. When it comes to cooking, there's more to a Mars Bar than just deep frying it!

Ingredients
- 2 Mars Bars, each about 60g, chopped
- 75ml single cream
- 200ml vodka

Method
1 Put the chopped Mars Bars and cream in a small saucepan over a low heat. Stir until the chocolate bars have melted and the mixture has combined.
2 Let the mixture cool then add in the vodka and stir very well.
3 Pour into a bottle and store in the fridge.
4 Shake well before serving, chilled from the fridge.

CHAPTER 6
DIRECTORY OF NATURAL INGREDIENTS

Enthusiastic liqueur makers often combine their infusions with a love of gardening or foraging, and of course in the days before refrigeration and freezing, bottling and preserving were the best ways of making the most of abundant seasonal ingredients.

Alexanders

Walk along any seaside path and you'll probably see this thriving, salt-tolerant edible plant growing. But these days it's not just a coastal plant, as it now grows more or less anywhere. It was a favourite with the Romans, who probably brought it to Britain from its Mediterranean homeland. It was much sought after at the time and was used in the same way celery or lovage might be. It was later commonly grown by monks and nuns and until the 19th century was also a common garden plant. Every part of it is edible and it also has medicinal uses. Its juices can be used to clean cuts and wounds and it's said to aid digestion.

Alexanders have been known to grow to more than 1.5m tall and can be recognised by their glossy green leaves with their toothed tips. They have many clusters of little yellow-green flowers that appear towards the top, suspended by offshoots from the main stem. Although the whole plant is edible it's the leaves that are usually used to make an infusion. The flavour is like a spicy, sharp celery, which makes it a perfect partner to a clean, clear spirit and for use in cocktails. For an even sharper, spicier flavour the roots and stems can be used. The seeds from the yellow flowers have a similar taste to coriander or cumin.

Apricots

A member of the plum (*prunus*) family, this scented, golden, exotic-looking fruit has been known of for more than 4,000 years and originally came from China. It now thrives in most temperate climates, which it prefers to tropical zones. The kernel, often known as the stone, can be used once roasted to make a liqueur, but most apricot infusions use just the fruit. The Italian liqueur amaretto is flavoured with extract of apricot kernels rather than almonds. The flesh ranges from a golden cream colour to a brilliant orange.

In Shakespeare's *A Midsummer Night's Dream*, Titania, the queen of fairies, tells her followers to feed apricots to Bottom, saying: 'Be kind and courteous to this gentleman. Hop in his walks and gambol in his eyes. Feed him with apricoks and dewberries.'

The flavour of apricots means it can be infused in darker spirits such as brandy and whisky and not just a clear spirit. If fresh fruit isn't available then dried fruits can be used too. Some infusers also try experimenting with a mixture of dry and fresh fruit. The dried fruit adds sweeter notes to the final drink.

Basil

Is there a more aromatic plant than basil? Sometimes known as Saint Joseph's wort, this member of the mint family is a native of the Mediterranean that is now also found throughout Asia and is widely grown in the UK. There are three main Mediterranean types: sweet, with large leaves; Greek, with smaller leaves and peppery and spicy notes; and purple, whose dark leaves have a milder flavour. Asian varieties include lemon basil; holy basil, spicy and intense; and Thai, similar to sweet basil but stronger.

If planted out in the UK the root dies as winter approaches, and therefore it must be sown anew every year. It can only survive the colder months if kept in a greenhouse.

It is widely thought to have many health benefits, including fighting against arthritis and inflammatory bowel disease. Some claim it can reduce swelling and has anti-ageing properties.

Basil's aromatic leaves make it ideal for use in infusions, especially in clear spirits. It also partners well with many other

ingredients, such as cucumbers. It is very much a summer flavour and a basil infusion is ideal for a long drink, poured over ice and garnished with a few fresh basil leaves.

Bilberries

Widely regarded as a superfruit, the bilberry is thought to lower blood pressure, regulate blood sugar levels and improve memory. Its anthocyanins are useful in improving eyesight and night-vision and in delaying the onset of cataracts. Perhaps this was why blueberry pie was popular with RAF pilots who wanted to improve their night vision during World War Two.

The fruit also works very well in infusions. A close relation to the blueberry, bilberries thrive on moorland, in hedgerows and on scrubland. The bushes easily grow up to 60cm in height, but are usually much smaller when they grow on rough moorland. Bilberry bushes have delicate red or sometimes white flowers that form the plant's blue-purple berries in the autumn. Bilberries have many common names including huckleberries, whortleberries, whinberries and, confusingly, blueberries. In France they're sometimes known as *myrtilles*.

The fruits grow as single, small berries and are a little darker and less juicy than true blueberries. They're easy to deep freeze, which makes them ideal for infusing at any time of the year.

In bilberry infusions the fruits are somewhat acidic, so be prepared to add sugar syrup to achieve the taste you're looking for. Bilberries also pair well with basil infusions.

Blackberries

There can't be many hedgerows or areas of scrubland that don't host blackberry plants. The black fruits of these sprawling, spiny bushes are a favourite for many foragers and are much sought after by country winemakers, pie makers, jam makers and infusers. Blackberry pickers are usually identified along roadsides or in parks by their fruit-stained fingers, and indeed lips, as they pick and sample these sweet, juicy fruits.

The seemingly impenetrable bushes are often called brambles, and consequently the fruits are sometimes called brambleberries. Other common names for them include dewberries, thimbleberries and lawyers (because it's hard to get away once they have their hooks in you!).

Strictly speaking a blackberry isn't a berry at all, but a collection of small round druplets, similar to a raspberry. According to folklore they shouldn't be picked after 11 October (Old Michaelmas Day), in case the Devil has spat on them. Others say the dark red juice of the berries is the blood

of Christ and the thorns of the bramble were used to make the crown of thorn worn at his crucifixion.

Ripe fruits can often be picked in late summer through September, and partner well with elderflower infusions.

Turning a hobby into a business

So can you turn your hobby into a business? Making infusions and liqueurs at home is a lot of fun, and you'll probably find that friends and family will tell you how much they enjoy your creations, especially if they've not had to pay for them. But praise isn't the same as a business plan.

Nevertheless, turning your hobby into a business is possible, though Ian McCulloch, a founding partner of Silent Pool Distillers, advises caution. Silent Pool was set up by a group of friends who had a passion for craft distilling and making infusions. They set up their distillery on the Duke of Northumberland's Albury Estate in Surrey, in a group of dilapidated farm buildings on the banks of the legendary Silent Pool.

According to McCulloch the big difference between a hobby and a business is that people making infusions at home for personal use don't have to deal with HMRC and therefore don't have access to the high-strength base spirits that are much more efficient at drawing the flavour from ingredients.

So it's possible, but not easy. 'The sectoral regulator is HM Revenue & Customs (HMRC), so that's your first hurdle,' says McCulloch. 'We infuse using 96% alcohol, whereas most hobbyists use shop-bought vodka at 40%. That's a key difference.'

The Little Red Berry Co in Ripon is also a hobby that turned into a business. It was set up in 2011 by Rachel and Rob Jamieson, and now makes many liqueurs including blackcurrant vodka, blackberry whisky and raspberry gin.

After ten years in the hospitality industry and vast experience in the UK and abroad, Rachel started the company following encouragement from those who'd tasted her delicious raspberry and sloe liqueurs. The company strives to source fruit locally from trusted growers to ensure the best quality ingredients, and there are no added colours or preservatives in any of their liqueurs or flavoured gins.

'We started with a small number of production tanks back in 2011 and now we've more than doubled our output,' says Rachel, 'so we were struggling for space.' The company therefore expanded into the unit next door to their original one, thereby creating more space without having to disrupt production.

'We're still very much a small-scale producer,' she says, 'and staying close to our roots is important to us. We started in a recession and there was no funding available at the time, so any growth we've done has been achieved organically.' Today the company produces approximately 18,000 bottles of liqueurs and gins annually by hand, in small batches. Its latest product is a London dry gin infused with a blend of elderflower and cucumber.

Blackcurrants

Blackcurrants readily grow in many gardens and allotments and produce bunches of dark purple to black fruits at midsummer. They have a tart flavour and provide an invaluable source of vitamin C. Blackcurrants grown as a domesticated crop are comparatively recent, occurring within the last 400–500 years, though they've probably been foraged for thousands of years. Healthy bushes are prolific producers of fruit, which is used to make pies, jams and cordials. Macerated blackcurrants are also the primary ingredient in the aperitif crème de cassis.

The fruits are usually available for picking from July to August. It is best to collect them on dry days, as wet berries can quickly go mouldy once picked. The fruit also freezes well. Once they're ripe it's best to pick them before fruit-eating birds discover and devour them.

Widely regarded as a superfruit, long before the term was first coined, blackcurrants have many health benefits. British herbals, dating as far back as the 17th century, refer to their

medicinal properties. The fruit's juice is high in oxidants, which when consumed fresh are said to reduce cancers. New studies also suggest that blackcurrant juice can play an important role in slowing the cognitive decline associated with ageing disorders, including dementia.

Cherries

The fruit is part of the family that also includes almonds, peaches, apricots and plums. They're small, fleshy, red or reddish-black fruits that contain a hard seed or 'pit' and can be divided into two broad groups – sweet and tart. Sweet cherries originated in Asia Minor in the fertile sweeping plains between the Black Sea and the Caspian. It's likely they were brought to Europe in the stomachs of migrating birds. The Greeks were the first to cultivate cherries and the Romans continued to increase and expand production.

The word cherry comes from the name of the Turkish town of Cerasus, while the name of the German cherry liqueur

kirsch derives from *karshu*, meaning 'cherry water', which was what cherries were called in ancient Mesopotamia when their cultivation commenced as far back as 8 BC.

Sweet or tart, fresh or frozen (but remember to defrost them!), they make a great ingredient for an infusion or liqueur. To add a little bitterness and a slight almond flavour, include a few of the pits. The rich flavours of cherry pair well with spices, so give cinnamon, allspice, cardamom or mace a go, and work well with a clear spirit such as vodka. Brandy is also worth trying, and it is even worth giving whisky and rum a go.

Sweet chestnuts

The Romans brought the sweet chestnut to Britain. The trees can live for 700 years and grow to 35m. Their edible nuts, which form inside a spiny husk, were an important source of food for centuries, as they can be ground into flour or coarse meal. Nutritionally they're very similar to wheat except for a lack of the protein gluten, a binding agent, so baked goods made with chestnut flour tend to have holes or a crumbly texture. Even today chestnuts are an important source of starch in parts of Europe, such as the island of Corsica, where they're also used to brew beer.

Alexander the Great and the Romans planted chestnut trees across Europe during their various campaigns. It's said that Roman soldiers were given a porridge made from sweet chestnuts before going into battle.

The ancient Greeks dedicated the sweet chestnut to Zeus, and its botanical name *Castanea sativa* comes from Castonis, a town in Thessaly where the tree was grown for its nuts.

Chillies

Chillies are a good way of adding a bit of heat to your infusions, and these colourful, tropical-looking plants are now widely grown in the UK. The heat or even sweetness in chillies comes from chemicals called capsinoids. There are different numbers of these molecules, which is why heat from different chillies is felt in different parts of the mouth. Contrary to popular belief the capsaicin in chillies isn't contained in the seeds, but rather in the fleshy strip inside the fruit to which the seeds are attached. When the cells containing the capsinoids are broken or sliced open they burst, spraying the chemical over the inside of the pod.

The heat of a chilli is traditionally measured in Scoville heat units (SHU), devised by scientist Wilbur Scoville in 1912. The principle is that a whole chilli is blended into sugar water and then diluted until it is no longer detectable by taste. The more sugar that has to be added, the hotter the chilli.

Hot chillies make a great addition to a good vodka, especially if you're a fan of a bloody Mary. The trick with using

warm or even fiery chillies is to get a balance between their heat and a pleasing, balancing sweetness. But chillies have a robust character that can add something to most spirits.

Coriander

Coriander, or 'cilantro' as Americans call it, is an annual plant that has edible leaves and seeds. It grows wild across Asia but can now be found worldwide, being famed for its spicy, aromatic leaves and seeds. People have been using it for many centuries – indeed, its seeds have even been found at Neolithic archaeological sites and in the tomb of Tutankhamun.

Fresh coriander leaves have a different taste from the seeds and are used by the handful in some recipes for their spicy overtones. The seeds have a much bigger orange, citrus flavour, and are a common ingredient in many beers, especially Belgian wheat-style beers. A gentle roasting of the dried seeds heightens their flavour and pungency. In some countries the roots are also used in sauces, because of their deep, intense flavours.

Seeds or leaves, coriander is an ideal partner to many other potential infusion ingredients, including the sharpness of lemon or the sweetness of elderflower.

Crab apples

A taste warning should probably be attached to crab apples, since, though there are a few sweet exceptions, most varieties are extremely sour due to their content of malic acid. However, they can make an interesting partner in an infusion, particularly in schnapps. The sweet variants are possibly the best to use, but the harder nature of the crab apple compared with eating varieties makes it a better ingredient for infusing, since most apples go mushy very quickly when used in infusions. Crab aple also works well in an infusion that includes cranberries, the tartness and sweetness of the fruits making for a refreshing, uplifting drink.

Crab apples play a big part in folklore and have long been associated with love and marriage. It was said that if you threw the pips into an open fire while saying the name of your love, the love would be true if the pips exploded like a firecracker. Apple wood was burned by the Celts during fertility rites and festivals, and Shakespeare makes reference to crab apples in *A Midsummer Night's Dream* and *Love's Labour's Lost*.

Crab apple trees can be found in some gardens but are more often a creature of the woods. They bloom in early to mid-spring, producing masses of pink, red or white flowers, depending on the variety, and produce hosts of small red or yellow fruits.

Cranberries

Cranberries make an intriguing infusion. Historically the cranberry was used medicinally, to treat wounds, diabetes, liver problems and stomach ailments. Today they are still recognised as being a nutritional and antibacterial powerhouse, high in vitamins and other good things. They are said to be beneficial for stomach, heart and dental health, kidney stones, yeast infections, cataracts, cognitive decline, cholesterol control and cancer prevention.

Most of the cranberries we use in Britain come from wetlands in the northern states of the USA, with Massachusetts being one of the best-known growing areas. Once these little red gems were picked slowly by hand, but today most are wet harvested.

Cranberries grow on low-lying vines in beds layered with sand, peat, gravel and clay, commonly known as bogs or marshes, and originally created by glacial deposits. In Massachusetts the cranberry farmers flood their bogs to protect plants from the freezing winter temperatures. The ice is then covered with sand, which is said to stimulate the growth of the plants. This practice dates back to the commercial beginnings of the industry, when in 1816 Captain Henry Hall of Dennis, Massachusetts, discovered that sand blowing on his cranberry vines stimulated their growth.

Today the growers of commercial bogs use a system of wetlands, uplands, ditches, flumes, ponds and other water bodies that provide a natural habitat for a variety of plant and animal life. So in the 1960s someone came up with the idea of flooding the bogs with water to help remove the berries

from the vines. The dry bogs are flooded with 40cm of water the night before the harvest. Then next day a flail-like device, nicknamed 'the Egg Beater', strips the berries off the plant and they float to the surface, since they have pockets of air inside them. The farmers then wade through the water 'corralling' the bobbing berries with booms so that they can be sucked or swept out of the water.

By contrast all you have to do is go into your supermarket and buy a packet, put them in the freezer overnight and then add a spirit.

Elderberries

It is with good reason that the elder, which can grow to up to 10m in height, is described as the queen of the hedgerows, since for part of the year it bears large clusters of beautiful white flowers. But for many people the plant comes into its own when the blossom turns to clusters of small, tart, black berries, which can be used to make a stunning infusion. And like many plants that seem to grow well close to people, the juice of its fruits is claimed to have many health benefits, including the power to fight colds, flu and some viruses. Well, they are full of anti-oxidants and Vitamin C! However, do remember that you want the black-berried version – the bright red variants are poisonous.

In some parts of Europe it is not uncommon to use schnapps rather than vodka or gin to make an elderberry infusion, sometimes served as an aperitif together with a spoonful of sugar to sweeten the taste. Another variant of the drink sees a few crushed cardamoms added to the infusion together with some slivers of lemon or orange peel.

For a sweet variant try a little honey, perhaps. Who knows, the bees might have already feasted on the sweet pollen of elderflowers.

Elderflowers

I don't know if elder trees really do ward off witches and spirits, but the straggly elder shrub does play a part in our pagan folklore. An elder bough placed by a door was said to ward off evil gremlins. Some people believe that wood from an elder should never be burnt. Perhaps that's because when alight it burns quickly and noisily – or could that be evil spirits escaping from their woody entrapment? And it is said that fairies played flutes made from twigs of dried and hollowed elder.

The fruits and the flowers of the elder are certainly important components of a number of alcoholic drinks. And since, as they say, a little of what you fancy does you good, there can't be too much wrong with the tree, whatever the mythology.

The delicate, white elderflowers explode into life in hedgerows, parks and roadsides in June, when the air seems to fill with the aroma of these exotic blooms. The best time to pick them is on a dry, warm day when the blooms are newly open. But be warned, it isn't just infusers or winemakers who are attracted to the flowers. Bugs love them. So it's best to give them a good shake as you pick them, and remember to wash them carefully before use.

Fennel

Fennel is a member of the carrot family. It comprises a white or pale green bulb from which closely intertwined, feathery leaves grow, and it is one of the most intriguing flavours people can easily grow in their garden. Bulb, stalk, leaves and seeds are all edible, the bulb being abundant with the flavours of warming aniseed. In France fennel is the key ingredient of a clear, aniseed-flavoured, ouzo-like drink called pastis, made from distilled grapes flavoured with aromatic herbs. Its name pastis is derived from *pastiche*, the word used to describe a drink introduced to replace absinthe when that was banned in many countries because of its alleged psychotropic effects.

Originating from the Mediterranean, fennel's tongue-tingling aniseed flavour comes from an aromatic chemical called anethole. The same flavour can also be found in star anise. Sweet to taste, you probably won't have to add sugar to this infusion.

In Italy a fennel liqueur is traditionally sipped after dinner, when the bottle is passed around the table until empty. Ambitious infusers might also add dill and fennel seeds to this drink.

Garlic

Fancy getting hot and spicy? Here's a drink that's not just for Halloween but for the whole year round. And if you use garlic grown in your own garden you'll probably create a drink of some piquancy. We've been using garlic for hundreds of years, if not longer, to add flavour to many food dishes. The garlic plant is in fact one of our oldest cultivated crops, and was fed to the builders of the Great Pyramid in Egypt in the belief that it gave them strength and endurance. In addition it's used in many traditional Indian and Chinese medicines as a remedy for colds, coughs and even bronchitis.

In modern medicine this member of the onion family is also valued for its anti-microbial, anti-cancer, anti-diabetic, immune system-boosting and cholesterol-lowering properties. It is said to be good for the heart, and if that isn't enough it's also said to fight off evil spirits and keep vampires away. A garlic infusion is the perfect partner to one of my favourite cocktails, the bloody Mary. And if you fancy giving it a bit of a smoked, sweet twist then add in some smoked or roasted garlic too. A hot variation is to add in a chilli for a spicy kick. Another variant is to partner basil with the garlic.

Gooseberries

Once every garden seemed to have gooseberry bushes growing in it. The fruit looks somewhat like a hairy, veined grape, but most gooseberry varieties are rarely as sweet. The fruits grow on spiky bushes, and pickers require adept fingers to pluck them without getting stabbed.

A member of the blackcurrant family, we've been eating them in Britain since the 16th century. They're the fruits of a temperate climate and are a good source of essential nutrients, including vitamin C, vitamin A, manganese and fibre. My mother often used them as an ingredient in a tart, but one of her crowning culinary creations was gooseberry fool, which is so simple to make; just simmer the fruit with a little sugar, chill, and fold in some whipped cream. Simple, affordable, and luxurious.

Sweet and sharp, a gooseberry infusion is really an English summer in a glass – sometimes sunny but often unpredictable. But that's the fun of this infusion. Many people who make it add some sugar syrup to sweeten it.

This is an infusion where it's often best to freeze the berries before using, as the skins will burst when defrosted. If not, top and tail the berries and cut them in half before putting into a jar and adding the spirit. Vodka would be my spirit of choice.

Gorse flowers

Is it just me, or does gorse seem to be in flower nearly all year around? Perhaps this is why there's an old saying that 'when gorse is out of blossom, kissing's out of fashion'. In some parts of the country the shrub is known as furze or whin.

The bright yellow flowers add colour to many a moor, but April is often the best time to see out these yellow flowers, which have a subtle aroma reminiscent of coconut. Our forebears would often add them to country wines, and it seems likely the petals would have been thrown into the mash tuns of long-gone brewers. Today some craft brewers in Denmark have added the flowers to a beer, and distillers in Ireland have added them to spirit.

A gorse bush grows about 2m high as a dense evergreen spiny shrub. A pair of gardening gloves is often useful when picking the flowers, and you need to be aware that bees love to seek nectar from gorse flowers.

At Southwestern Distillery in Cornwall they produce a modern take on French anise by taking foraged gorse flowers and adding fresh orange zest 'to help deliver its fresh, invigorating and unique aroma'. The company's distiller says the gorse flowers give the infusion some wonderful coconut notes.

Haws

The small red fruits of the hawthorn comprise a large stone surrounded by a creamy-white flesh that's very slightly sweet but often has a bitter aftertaste when eaten raw. Together with hawthorn leaves they've been widely used throughout history to produce therapeutic medications. Kidney stones, heart disease and respiratory illnesses are all said to be cured by the use of haws, and some Chinese herbalists use them to improve the body's blood flow.

Once one of the three sacred trees of the Celts, the hawthorn is a large bush or deciduous tree with branches that are protected by large thorns. In some parts of the country the plant is often called 'bread and cheese', because that's what the leaves taste like.

The red berries are usually produced in clusters and can be eaten raw or used for a jam. In addition they make a fantastic partner to a spirit. To draw the maximum flavour from the small, almost miniature apple-like fruits, it is best to freeze them overnight and defrost them before marrying with a spirit.

A member of the rose family, hawthorn is also called whitethorn because of the whiteness of its bark, and the fruit or haws are called by many interesting names, such as pixie pears and cuckoo's beads. The German name for hawthorn is *hagedorn*, which means 'hedge thorn', indicating that it was used to mark boundaries between fields.

Mint

Mint, which can seem to grow rampantly in many a garden or allotment, is one of the most aromatic plants available to the infuser. It comes in many flavours, including peppermint, apple mint, spearmint, lavender mint and even ginger mint. It is a member of a large family of herbs that includes basil, rosemary, sage, oregano and catnip.

Mint is said to promote digestion and is a great flavour enhancer. Perhaps that's why it pairs with lamb, helping cut through the meat's fatty texture. It's also said to soothe stomachs in cases of indigestion or inflammation. More importantly, mint is an ingredient of one of the world's greatest cocktails, the mint julep. A favourite in southern US states, particularly Kentucky, this drink is a mixture of bourbon, sugar syrup, mint leaves and crushed ice. The classic version is served in silver julep cups.

Perhaps because of the deceptive strength of its flavour it makes a great partner to many spirits, and not just vodka. Whisky, rum, gin and schnapps are all enhanced by an infusion of mint leaves. For the best results I've always found

Cath Harries

that the infusing time should be shorter rather than longer. For me a couple of days is always best. Left longer the infusion can turn a muddy brown if used with a clear spirit.

Nettles

The hairs on a nettle's leaves might have a vicious sting when brushed with a bare arm or leg, but their contribution to infusions is far less painful. My mother often used the heads of nettles as the basis of a wine and swore blind that the leaves could be boiled and eaten in a similar way to spinach. I've never tried eating them, but have drunk a beer that's been made with an addition of hops to the kettle. And there's a rather nice cheese which is flavoured with nettle leaves.

The nettle has many uses by those who advocate herbal infusions. The plant is said to be good for a variety of conditions, including anaemia, osteoarthritis, various allergies and hay fever. So, like many of our garden weeds it has many positive attributes. If making a spirited infusion with it, it's best to use the tops of young nettles. Do pick carefully to ensure that you don't get stung. In fact it's probably best to wear garden gloves.

In Scandinavia and Germany some people make schnapps flavoured with young, fresh nettle leaves and stems. The drink has a pleasing, aromatic taste with an intriguing hint of bitterness. The infusion starts off a bold, fresh green colour but can turn a reddish hue if left too long. But don't worry, that shouldn't affect the taste.

Plums

Could our ancestors have first used the phrase 'picking the low-hanging fruit' when they discovered ripe plums? It certainly seems likely, since this stoned fruit is said to have been one of the first cultivated by humans. And with good reason, as a ripe plum is full of such marvellous, nutritious, sweet flavours.

Plums have so many uses. They can be eaten fresh, the flesh can be turned into a jam, the juice can make fulsome wine, or they can be baked into cakes, tarts, pies and crumbles. Dried into prunes they provide nutrients over the winter, and have garnered a reputation for laxative qualities. In some parts of the world they are dried, salted and eaten as a snack, and salted plum has also been mixed with ground liquorice and used as an ingredient in cocktails. In the Balkans they love to infuse plums in brandy, creating a fragrant, smooth drink. But the depth of flavour of plums means that they'll work with most spirits. The fruits can be cut and the stones removed or the whole fruit can be put into the infusion. I've tried it both ways with good results.

Once you're happy with the taste of your infusion, strain it well. Don't throw the fruit away – it's too good to waste and can be used in a trifle or a pie.

Plum'ing marvellous

Set on the banks of the River Spey in picturesque Moray, the Gordon Castle Estate is the spiritual home of the Gordon Clan, and at over eight acres its famed walled garden is one of Scotland's largest and oldest.

Walled kitchen gardens are an important part of our history, yet are now largely neglected and little understood. For centuries most large country houses and monasteries had a walled kitchen garden. They were highly productive places, supplying food, herbs and flowers. The high walls provided protection from predators and the elements and created a unique microclimate within. Heat retained by the walls helped in the production of fruit on trees trained against them. Many also had glasshouses within them, where the growing season could be extended and exotic species of herbs and spices could be produced.

In their heyday in the Victorian and Edwardian eras such gardens provided an abundance of fruit, vegetables, and herbs. Many soft fruits have been grown within Gordon Castle's own walled garden, and currently 249 espaliered fruit trees line its walls.

The garden has recently been fully restored and a new gin, distilled by Gordon & MacPhail, contains botanicals from some of the 4,000 plants now grown there. The eponymously named Gordon Castle plums are amongst the fruits and herbs used to make this infusion, which is described as crisp, elegant and refreshing, with a clean palate and subtle notes of lavender and peppermint. The estate's raspberries go into another infusion. Interestingly only 40 raspberries are used for each bottle of gin, so it's a fine example of little being more.

The current custodian of the castle, Angus Gordon Lennox, explains: 'As with all of our products, history and heritage is at the heart of our story. The plums that make this liqueur truly unique were developed at Gordon Castle over a century ago when my forbears owned the Estate. I remember as a boy spending the summer months playing in our garden surrounded by 300 espaliered fruit trees, so the fact that we can still produce enough plums to make this limited edition gin liqueur is a credit to the dedicated gardeners who've cared for the land for centuries.'

To enjoy his liqueurs to full advantage he recommends drinking them on their own or mixed with a splash of sparkling white wine.

For more information visit http://www.gordoncastlescotland.com/gin/.

Raspberries

Raspberries are another taste of English summer – soft, sweet and short-lived. I remember the raspberries on my parents' long rows of fruit canes. Cut back to the ground each winter, they'd burst into life again every spring and by the summer would be heavy with fruit. The harvest season always seemed too short and was a battle between eager hands, hungry birds and sudden rainstorms that could strip the fruit from the plants.

Today new varieties see the harvest time for raspberries extended from the end of spring well into autumn. However, that's done nothing to dull the excitement of picking these little clusters of sweetness.

A handful or two of these fruits will make a joyous contribution to an infusion. It doesn't take a clear spirit to draw the colour and flavours from freshly picked raspberries. Within a few days – certainly no more than ten – you'll have a drink that seems to catch the flavours of a summer's day. This fast infusion will need little more than a good sieving before bottling.

If colour is important in a cocktail, then this infusion with its natural sweetness is an ideal component. Add a little sugar syrup to it, carefully, to get the taste you're looking for and you'll have a liqueur of some distinction.

Rhubarb

Does every allotment have a clump of rhubarb? They certainly seem to be the eternal perennial of many vegetable plots. Probably because growing rhubarb has to be one of the easiest things for even the most ungreen-fingered gardener to do. In fact growing rhubarb is so easy that it has even gained a reputation for thriving on neglect. The leaves of the plant grow big, and indeed are poisonous as they contain oxalic acid, but it's the pink-red stems that infusers seek.

The season for rhubarb can last many weeks, often from April to July, but an added bonus of the plant is that the stems freeze well, which means that a supply can be put into a deep freeze ready for whenever you want to make your infusion.

For the best infusion the stems should be cut into pieces 2–3cm in length and covered with the spirit of your choice. My preference is vodka. It's also best to make sure you have some sugar syrup available when you're ready to bottle, as the plant – despite its distinctly sweet taste – has little inherent sugar. Just add enough of the syrup to achieve the sweetness you want.

Some like to drink this infusion short on its own, but it is transformed when mixed with a soda or lemonade, when it becomes a long drink of some excellence.

After a month of infusing the stems in a dark place, don't throw them away when they've been strained off. If you like the idea of a boozy fruit pie or crumble, then these are an ideal ingredient.

Rose hips

Rose hips are a taste from my childhood. In Britain they were once widely used to make a sweet, nutritious syrup, and during World War Two the Government distributed recipes to make rose hip syrup at home. I have a memory of being given a spoonful of rose hip syrup each day in winter. 'It's good for you,' I was told. Well, it does have more vitamin C than oranges, and it's jammed with lots of other vitamins and antioxidants. However, it wasn't until later years that I discovered that an adult version was made using vodka or gin.

Unsurprisingly, the rose hip – also known as a rose haw or rose hep – is the fruit of the rose plant. If you have a rose bush or tree in your garden, then come autumn you'll have them in abundance. They can also be found in plentiful quantities growing wild as briars in hedgerows. They begin to form on the plant after successful pollination of the flowers in spring or early summer, and they ripen in late summer through to autumn.

Recipes traditionally recommend picking the hips after a frost. However, these days putting the fruits in a freezer overnight before use achieves the same result. In some parts of Eastern Europe the rose hips are mixed with brandy. In Hungary, for

instance, some of the recipes for an infusion called palinka use rose hips, though a variety of herbs and fruits can be used. The drink is said to aid digestion and is imbibed from small glasses after a large meal.

Rosemary

The earthy, citrus-like fragrance of rosemary has graced many gardens, kitchens and infusions. It is a herb of the Mediterranean that nevertheless prospers well in our temperate climate. The flat, pine-like leaves touched with silver are filled with a beautiful oily, aromatic essence.

It has a thousand uses, one of which is that it seems to be the natural partner of roasted lamb. Ancient chemists used it to improve people's memories, and it is said to lower blood pressure, combat infection and fight against cancer. The herb is also a marvellous partner to vodka, an affinity it shares with lavender. The resultant flavoured vodka is a wonderful addition to homemade cocktails.

A rosemary infusion is very easy to make. Put a few sprigs into a small jar, cover them with vodka and leave the jar in a dark place for a good week. It's best to use fresh rosemary rather than dried – which will work, however, if that's all you have available, though the results aren't normally as good. The infusion seems to taste best if the sprigs are picked at the beginning of the summer, when they're full of vibrant flavours. The taste becomes a little woody if the leaves are picked later.

If you're looking for an alternative to vodka, then add a few sprigs of rosemary to some gin. Leave to infuse for

at least three days, then strain the spirit off and you have a drink of some distinction. Try pairing it with a favourite tonic, especially one that pairs with rosemary, garnish with a little cucumber and a sprig of rosemary or even basil, then sip and enjoy. It's a classic.

Rose petals

Roses have a long and colourful history. In one of the bloodiest periods of England's history the red rose of Lancaster and the white rose of York were the symbols of two warring families. Fossil evidence of the plant dating back more than 35 million years has been found, and people have probably been cultivating it for more than 5,000 years. As with many plants that help define civilisations, it is thought this first happened in China. Rich Romans established rose gardens in various lands of conquest and settlement.

Rose water, a scented infusion made by steeping the petals in water, has been used as a beauty treatment and a flavouring in cooking for centuries, in Middle Eastern, Indian and Chinese traditions. The gorgeous flavour of the Middle Eastern pastry baklava results from the use of rose water, and the best rose water was once so valuable it was used as a form of currency. Rose water is also the main ingredient of Turkish delight.

The addition of fresh rose petals to a spirit creates an infusion of aromatic complexity. The petals can be picked from your own garden or even from briars growing wild. They don't need to be steeped for too long and it is unlikely that you'll want to add sugar to it.

I've never tried it, but I've heard of people who, once they've strained the infused spirit off the petals, use them to make a boozy tea. Now that's something I'd like to try one day.

Sage

Every kitchen garden or plot growing mixed herbs probably has sage growing in it somewhere. It is a sister plant to rosemary and mint, other herbs which also make ideal spirit partners.

Like many plants derived from the Mediterranean, it was widely used by the Greeks and the Romans, who wondered at its health-giving properties. It was also used as a preservative, and the oils in its leaves are reputed to enhance people's brainpower. According to some reports Arab physicians in the 10th century believed that it even promoted immortality, though sadly none of them are alive today to ask if it worked.

It has been used to treat sprains, swellings and ulcers. It was supposed to cure coughs and sneezes, strengthen the nervous system and sharpen people's senses. Europeans in the Middle Ages used it to protect themselves from witchcraft, and in the 17th century sage was so highly valued by Chinese merchants that they would exchange three chests of China tea for one of sage from Dutch merchants.

Sage adds a peppery, savoury note to a spirit infusion. A few sprigs of sage in some vodka, which is left to infuse for a few days, makes a great addition to a red wine sangria. Served over ice with lots of fruit it is the perfect drink for a long summer's afternoon in the sun.

Sea buckthorn

According to legend it was sea buckthorn that made Genghis Khan and his army strong. The ancient Greeks are said to have fed it to their horses during the winter months. Perhaps that's why it was the preferred food of the fabled flying horse Pegasus. Widely regarded as an important plant because of its healing properties, its berries have been used for generations to prepare homemade cosmetics, cure various infections and heal wounds.

Sea buckthorn is a deciduous small shrub that can grow as tall as 4m. It has rough brown bark and a thick, greyish-green crown made up of spiky green leaves. But it is the yellow-gold berries we're interested in. These have been used for centuries against colds, fever, exhaustion, as an analgesic or as a treatment for stomach ulcers, cancer and metabolic disorders. The oil from the berries is also used in hair products.

Tart to taste, the berries once infused often benefit from the addition of a little sugar syrup. If infused in vodka they produce a copper-coloured liqueur with earthy aromas of honey, soy and wheat. This can be sampled on its own but also makes a perfect foil for a creative cocktail. Like most infusions made from hard fruits, freezing the berries before infusion is usually best.

Sloe

These astringent little blue berries will pair with most spirits – vodka, whisky and even tequila work well with sloes.

The fruit of the blackthorn bush, a member of the plum family, sloes are very small, green-fleshed, inky-skinned wild plums with a tart flesh and bitter skin. They are usually found in hedgerows, indeed there can't be a hedgerow in England, Scotland, Wales or Ireland that doesn't have a blackthorn bush!

Fans of sloe infusions relish a cool, wet summer, as then the fruits ripen sooner, which means that you won't have to wait until the first frosts before they can be harvested. Pick them when they feel ripe and place in a freezer before use.

Sloes picked in the autumn will be ready to drink by Christmas. They can also be used to make a wine, jelly, jam, ice cream or syrup, and can be added to many dishes. And have fun devising you own cocktails: add some orange zest, cloves or a little bit of cinnamon. What could be better? A dark liqueur, with an alluring sweetness. It has to be tried.

Strawberries

In Roman times wild strawberries were said to cure melancholy, fainting, gout, blood diseases and even bad breath. The distribution of wild strawberries is largely from seeds that have been through a bird's gut. Wherever fruit-eating birds have flown, strawberries have followed. The fruit has been widely cultivated since the 18th century and its popularity continues to grow. Like many of our modern varieties of fruit, today's strawberries are the result of a cross between species from both sides of the Atlantic. In particular English plant breeders did most of the early crossbreeding work to develop the ancestors of the varieties we enjoy today.

A strawberry infusion is very easy. Halve or quarter the fruits, cover with the spirit of your choice – I've found that vodka is best – then keep in a dark cupboard for three or four days. Strain, and the job's nearly done. On tasting you might feel want to add some sugar syrup. This simple process will leave you with a fragrant and naturally sweet vodka. It can be sipped on its own or used as an ingredient in a cocktail.

Strawberries also partner particularly well with other fruits and herbs, so the addition of some sprigs of basil or a chilli to the vodka at the same time as the strawberries will produce an interesting infusion.

Walnuts

Walnuts are one of the oldest tree fruits known, and records in Persia date them back to 7000 BC. So valuable were the nuts that they were regularly traded and used as a currency on the Silk Road, the ancient trading route between Asia and the Middle East.

The Romans probably brought walnut trees to England. Great Britain is at the northern limit of the tree's preferred climate zone. However, the walnut tree has two important attributes, for in addition to its annual prodigious supply of nutritious nuts the timber is ideal for furniture-making and was more valuable than oak.

In France and parts of Italy a favourite walnut liqueur is nocino, which is made from green walnuts before the outer husk has hardened. These days unripe fresh green walnuts aren't easy to come by, unless you're lucky enough to have a walnut tree growing in your garden. But for this recipe you can also use a handful of chopped walnuts bought from a supermarket or health food shop. Either cut the unripe walnuts into quarters or lightly crush the dried nuts then cover with a spirit of your choice – vodka works well, but so does brandy – and leave for four weeks.

It's likely that the resultant infusion will be cloudy. That won't do you any harm, but it's probably best to strain it very well. Finally add sugar syrup to suit your taste – it usually doesn't need much.

Wormwood

As we've already seen, wormwood is the key ingredient of one of the world's best-known alcoholic drinks – absinthe. A key component of the ingredient is its bitterness, which is perhaps why it's a common ingredient in many digestifs, including vermouth.

The Latin name of the plant is *Artemisia*, which comes from the name of the Greek goddess Artemis, who protected women during childbirth. Even today some herbalists say the plant will relieve morning sickness, prevent miscarriage, soothe earaches and ear infections and treat obesity. In the Middle Ages it was also used to kill tapeworms without injuring their human host.

Its leaves were once used to spice mead, an alcoholic drink made from honey, and medieval brewers may have used them as a substitute for or in addition to hops. Recently several brewers in England have made beers using wormwood, while in Poland a vodka macerated with wormwood leaves can be found. Called Piołunowka, it is a very bitter glass full.

Sometimes called mugwort, wormwood is a woody perennial sub-shrub noted for its fragrant, silvery foliage and tolerance of poor growing conditions. The plant can be found in many gardens. A wormwood infusion is simple to make. Take a few sprigs of the leaves and cover with vodka or gin. Leave in a dark place for a few days and add sugar syrup to taste.

CHAPTER 7
MAKE YOUR
OWN LIQUEURS

Selected recipes

In this chapter we present a selection of recipes that make a good starting point in becoming an accomplished creator of your own liqueurs. Use them as a guide rather than a blueprint and feel free to experiment and adapt, according to your personal taste and preferences. Start with small quantities and keep a record of the results.

ARTICHOKE GIN

If you like your vodka bitter then this could be the infusion for you. Artichokes are the main component of a commercial Italian bitter known as Cynar. However, these edible thistles are only one of the actors that go into the production of the drink – at least a dozen other botanicals are used – which is an essential for anyone who likes a twist on the classic Negroni cocktail.

The name of the drink derives from *Cynar scolymus*, the botanical name for the artichoke, as artichoke leaves lend it its distinctive flavour. One of the interesting side-effects of tasting cynarin, the active chemical component in the leaves, is that most things you taste after it are sweeter. Perhaps this is why it's such a popular digestive for serving before dinner.

Ingredients
- 250ml gin or vodka
- 4–5 artichoke leaves
- Lemon zest (optional)
- Sugar syrup, to taste (optional)

Method
1 Wash and dry the artichoke leaves and chop very finely.
2 Put the chopped leaves into your container and cover with your chosen spirit. Add in lemon zest if required. Leave in a dark place for a week.
3 Taste and add sugar syrup if necessary. Strain very well and bottle.

BACON-INFUSED VODKA

There can't be many people who don't like the smell of frying or grilling bacon. But using bacon in an infusion? Well, if there's one ingredient the home infuser must try at least once it's bacon. And if you like your drinks hot then you can add a bit of spice by putting in some chillies. The resultant infusion should be a perfect base for a hot bloody Mary, a perfect start to a late brunch.

If you are using about 250ml of vodka you'll need one or two slices of uncooked bacon and a couple of fresh chillies. The chillies are optional and their colour and heat are entirely up to you, but as this infusion is best used as a building block for the perfect bloody Mary you should make it hot and spicy. An interesting variant is to use whisky instead of vodka.

Ingredients
- 2 slices of bacon
- 1–2 red chillies, cut in half and deseeded
- 250ml vodka

Method
1 Grill or fry the bacon until it is crispy then place it on a piece of kitchen towel and let it cool.
2 Add the split seeded chillies and the cold bacon to your container and top up with vodka. Seal the container and pop into a fridge.
3 Taste after three days and if it is hot enough for you then

strain very well and discard the chillies and bacon. If you like a little more heat, then steep for another three days or so. Then strain thoroughly. The infusion might need straining more than once. Once bottled, store in a fridge.
4 If you think the infusion is too spicy, don't worry. If you're using it in a bloody Mary the infusion's fiery tones will be subdued by the addition of tomato juice. Serve the bloody Mary garnished with a rasher of crispy bacon.

BEETROOT VODKA

Anyone who's had an allotment has probably grown beetroot. And anyone who's grown beetroot has probably wondered what to do with it – there is only so much borsch a family can eat. However, while a spirited infusion is unlikely to reduce by much any beetroot glut you might have, it will create a drink that's likely to spark interest among family and friends.

Beetroot-infused vodka makes an interesting base to a spicy bloody Mary, or you could try it neat, well-chilled and served over ice.

Ingredients
- 250ml vodka
- 1 small/medium cooked beetroot, chopped
- Small piece of fresh horseradish (optional)
- Sugar syrup, to taste (optional)

Method
1 Put the chopped beetroot into your container and cover with vodka. To give the drink a bit of a hot kick, add in a small piece of fresh horseradish root.
2 Give the container a good shake then put into a dark place for three or four days.
3 Filter out the beetroot pulp and horseradish, if used, through a muslin-lined sieve or paper filter.
4 Taste the beetroot and add sugar syrup to taste. Leave in a dark place for a week or so. Filter and bottle. The spirit-infused beetroot can be mixed with some yoghurt or lightly beaten double cream and served with a slice of fresh ham.

BLACKBERRY CHILLI GIN

This liqueur can be drunk on its own, made into a long drink with ice and tonic, or drizzled over ice cream or vanilla cheesecake. My thanks to the Dartmoor Chilli Farm for the recipe.

Ingredients

- 1kg blackberries
- 500g golden caster sugar
- 300ml gin
- 3 chilli pods (mild/medium heat – Cayenne Long Slim is a good option)
- 1 cinnamon stick

Method

1 Wash and dry the blackberries. In a blender, add the blackberries, chillies and 125g of the sugar and blitz until puréed.
2 Strain the mix through a sieve into a pan.
3 Add the rest of the sugar and the cinnamon stick to the pan and simmer for about 15 minutes until the sugar has dissolved. Then add the gin and stir in.
4 Remove from the heat and take out the cinnamon stick.
5 Strain the mix through the sieve again into a jug (this is to remove any final stray seeds). Pour into sterilised bottles and seal.
6 Store in a dark place for a few weeks before using. This gives the flavours time to mature. Serve straight with ice, or with tonic and a sprig of mint.

BLACKCURRANT CHILLI BRANDY

Thanks to the Dartmoor Chilli Farm for this recipe too, which teams chillies and dark berries with brandy for a deliciously rich liqueur.

Ingredients

- 1kg blackcurrants
- 600ml brandy
- 2–3 red chillies
- 400g sugar

Method

1 Wash and strip the blackcurrants off their stems.
2 Put blackcurrants, chillies and sugar into a blender and roughly blend for 10–20 seconds.
3 Tip the mush into a 1.5-litre preserving jar (sterilised) and pour the brandy over the top.
4 Seal the jar then store in a cool dark place, shaking the jar every few days.
5 After two months pour the liquid through a sieve lined with muslin into a sterilised jug.
6 Pour into sterilised bottles, seal, label and store in a cool dark place prior to use.

CARDAMOM VODKA

Cardamom is one of the oldest and most expensive spices in the world and it changed the taste of European cooking. It's a member of the ginger family and originates from India, Pakistan and Nepal. Its leaves and seeds can both be used in cooking. The leaves have a fresh, sweet note with hints of wood, cinnamon and salt and make a really interesting infusion.

Ingredients
- 1g cardamom leaves – a couple of cardamom pods could be used if leaves aren't available
- 250ml gin/vodka
- ½ vanilla pod (optional)

Method
1 Lightly crush the leaves, put into your container and cover with the vodka.
2 Leave to infuse in a dark place for seven days.
3 Taste the drink and if it is strong enough strain and bottle. If you want a stronger flavour add in some more leaves and leave for a few more days.

4 For a variation you could try adding in part of a vanilla pod.
5 Drink it neat or make it long with ice, tonic, sugar syrup, sliced lemon or limes, and a vanilla pod as the finishing touch, if you wish.

CELERY INFUSION

Celery is one of those plants that's subject to what I call the Marmite effect – people either love it or hate it. The stems have a sharp, tangy taste. In particular, the inner stems and heart of a celery plant are particularly tasty.

A stick of celery has become an essential component of the bloody Mary cocktail, though this wasn't always so. When the cocktail was first invented in the 1920s it didn't include celery, but in the 1960s a customer in a Chicago hotel is said to have wanted something to stir his drink. He took a stick of celery off the salad bar, and the rest, as they say, is history.

Vodka infused with celery makes an interesting drink on its own and is also a useful infusion for any cocktail maker to have in their repertoire.

Ingredients
- 250ml vodka
- 1 stick or a heart of celery, washed and trimmed
- 5 peppercorns, lightly crushed (optional)

Method
1 Using a grater or a mandolin, cut up the celery and put into your container.
2 Add in the peppercorns if you're using them. Cover with vodka and leave to infuse for five days in a dark place.
3 Taste, and if you're happy with it strain and bottle.
4 If you prefer a stronger flavour add in some more grated celery and leave for a couple more days.

CLOVE INFUSION

The bridge between medicine and flavoursome spices seems to be bridged by the clove. Many people who've had a toothache might well have taken a tincture of cloves to salve the pain. And lovers of curries or baked apple will also, no doubt, have tasted this distinctive spice.

Cloves are the rich, brown, dried unopened flower buds of an evergreen tree belonging to the myrtle family. Their name comes from the Latin word *clavus*, meaning nail.

Originating from the Molucca Islands, now part of Indonesia, cloves have been used for thousands of years. One of the earliest references to them says that the Chinese, before being permitted to approach the emperor, had to have a few cloves in their mouths to sweeten the breath.

Today cloves are not just two a penny but probably ten, but once upon a time they were very costly in Europe, and countries fought wars to protect their supply of them, since in an era before refrigeration cloves helped flavour food that was past its best. Consequently huge fortunes were made by companies importing cloves from Asia into Europe. The glittering wealth of the Portuguese and Spanish courts, of Italian port cities and German, Dutch and British traders, was down to spices like the clove.

A clove-infused spirit is quite strong-tasting, with spicy, aromatic and medicinal notes. It's one of those drinks that makes you think, 'I'm glad I tried that' and then confine it to the dustbin of history. But cloves are often added to the botanicals that are poured into gin and schnapps, so it's a spice which should be given time. And you might find it works better if used together with other ingredients such as citrus zest and cinnamon.

Ingredients
- ■ 250ml vodka
- ■ 12 cloves
- ■ 1 cinnamon stick
- ■ 1 strip of peeled grapefruit zest

Method
1 Put the cloves into your container and cover with vodka.
2 Leave for a few days before tasting, straining and bottling. If you're not happy with it, leave for a couple more days.
3 Serve on ice with fresh grapefruit juice, soda water and a cinnamon stick.

DAMSON GIN

September is said to be the best month to pick these little gems. The small, dark fruits, which are a member of the prune family, are a very English fruit. They were grown not just for their petite fleshy plums but also their juice, which was used as a dye. (Beware spilling a damson infusion on a white tablecloth!) Until the 1940s damsons were found on most dining tables, since the use of large amounts of sugar transformed the sour, tart fruits for use in delicious jams and cheeses. The name is said to derive from the city of Damascus, and it's likely that as with many other fruits they were brought to these shores by the Romans.

Once there were many damson orchards in Britain and they're still commercially grown in small quantities. It's also not unusual to find a tree growing wild or in a garden on land that was once used as an orchard.

Traditionally, when making an infusion with gin or vodka the little plums would be pricked and packed into a glass with what seems like kilos of sugar before being covered with spirit and then left for a long time, waiting for the sugar grains to dissolve. Many traditional recipes call for 500g of sugar for every 500g of fruit! The resultant liqueur would be vibrant in colour and sweet. Very, very sweet.

Today, rather than pricking them it is easier to freeze the damsons. Then when you take them out of the freezer they split naturally. Using sugar syrup after prime maceration speeds up the whole process of the sugar dissolving and gives the infuser much more control over the drink's final sweetness.

When the infusion has been strained, don't throw the fruit away. De-stone and dry it in a very low oven for a couple of hours. It can then be used in cakes or puddings.

The recipe below is for 'old style' damson gin like your grandmother or even your grandfather might have made. Modern variations are usually not as sweet and don't take so long.

Ingredients

- 450g damsons
- 450g sugar
- 750ml gin
- Sugar syrup, to taste (optional)

Method

1 Wash and dry the damsons, freeze or prick each one before placing into a clean container. Add the sugar, replace the lid and shake hard until the sugar is very pink.

2 Pour in the gin, shake again, and store in a dark place. Turn and swill the fruit around once a day until the sugar has dissolved, then leave and shake only occasionally.

3 After three months, taste, adding a little sugar syrup if you need to, then strain and bottle.

DANDELION VODKA

Many herbalists get excited when they see dandelions in flower, but the vibrant yellow flowers give heart palpitations to any gardener trying to create the perfect lawn. It doesn't matter how often the plants are cut down, they always seem to grow back. The herbalist, however, doesn't see a problem, just a plant that can lower blood pressure and cleanse the body of toxic material. Indeed, it seems there's very little the dandelion can't do, as it's also supposed to offer relief from liver disorders, diabetes, urinary disorders, acne, jaundice, cancer and anaemia. It also helps maintain healthy bones and skin.

The flowers are best picked on a bright sunny day. A childhood memory is of my parents gathering hundreds of the flowers in order to make a sweet wine.

The name dandelion comes from the French word *dent de lion,* meaning 'lion's tooth', referring to the plant's coarsely-toothed leaves. Dandelions have one of the longest flowering seasons of any plant and according to some reports our forebears would rather have a lawn of these plants than grass. Which is hardly surprising, as every part of the dandelion is useful and can be used for food, medicines and dye. It also makes an interesting infusion, with a sweet, almost peppery note.

Ingredients
■ Dandelion flowers
■ Vodka
■ Sugar syrup, to taste (optional)

Method
1 Wash the dandelion flowers then spread on kitchen paper until completely dry. With a knife, remove the green base of the flowers.
2 Fill approximately one third of your container with the flowers and then fill the bottle with vodka. Close the jar.
3 Store in a cool, dark place for three to five days.
4 Strain, and add sugar syrup if needed, then bottle and label.

HONEY WHISKY

Honey is just honey, isn't it? No, this gift from the millions of bees in hives comes in a variety of textures and flavours. Clover honey is probably the most common and also the mildest in taste, and if you use it in an infusion you could have a bit of fun by adding in some extra flavourings – perhaps a vanilla pod, cinnamon, star anise or the zest of an orange or lemon. Just think of what goes well with honey and it'll probably work in your infusion.

However, a walk through a farmers' market will probably reveal lots of artisanal honey makers. The colour, flavour and even the aroma of a particular variety of honey may differ depending on the nectar source of the flowers visited by the bees. And depending on your preferences you might find that a stronger honey, say one made from heather flowers, doesn't need the addition of any other flavourings.

Ingredients
■ 250ml whisky
■ 1 tbsp honey
■ 1 tbsp just-boiled water
■ Citrus zest, vanilla pod or star anise (optional)

Method
1 Mix the honey with an equal amount of boiled water until disolved.
2 Pour the solution into your container, add the whisky and any other optional ingredients, if using, seal and shake.
3 Leave for 12 hours or so, then strain if necessary.
4 Bottle, and it's ready to drink.

FIG INFUSION

Like many of our fruits that are commonly available worldwide, figs are thought to have originated on the fertile plains of Northern Asia. Its fruit was the food of the Greek gods, and Plato documented that Greek athletes at Olympia were fed diets of figs to increase their running speed and overall strength. The sugar-rich fruits even get a mention in the New Testament, Jesus condemning a fig tree for not producing any fruit for him as he passed by, a curse that killed the tree.

Thankfully there are many other trees still producing the rich, luscious fruits that have been used to sweeten food since ancient times. Hardly surprising, since figs contain 50% sugar.

Infusing figs in a spirit is ridiculously easy, and the flavour, aroma and colour of figs means that they're an ideal partner to most spirits. They work very well in vodka, but equally have the necessary depth of character to work well with the fulsome flavours of a brandy or whisky.

Ingredients
■ 250ml spirit of your choice – vodka, whisky or brandy
■ 2–3 ripe figs
■ Sugar syrup, to taste (optional)

Method
1 Rinse and dry the figs, quarter them, put them into your container and cover with spirit. Leave for about five days, remembering to shake most days.
2 Taste. If you aren't happy with the level of figginess leave for a few more days and if the infusion isn't sweet enough add a little sugar syrup. Strain well and bottle. Try serving on crushed ice, topped with lemonade and garnished with sliced fresh figs.

MANGO RUM

The mango is thought to have originated over 5,000 years ago in Asia, and, like many plants discovered by Europeans in the 16th century, its propagation around the world has followed the old spice trade routes. The Portuguese, who landed in Calcutta in 1498, were the first to establish a mango trade. Today the evergreen tree that fruits mangos is grown in tropical and subtropical countries everywhere, from South-East Asia to South America.

The mango has to be one of the most aromatic of exotic fruits and is very sweet. It seems to benefit form a drizzle of acidity to bring out the fulsomeness of its flavours.

Ingredients
■ 250ml white rum
■ 1 mango
■ A small strip of lime or lemon zest (optional)
■ Sugar syrup, to taste (optional)

Method
1 Cut and peel a mango and put about half the fruit in your container. Cover with rum and add the lemon or lime zest. Shake the mixture and leave in a dark place for 4–5 days.
2 Shake and taste, and if you think it needs it, add a little sugar syrup. Leave to mature for another week or so. The taste will become more concentrated the longer you leave it.
3 Strain very well – it might also need to be filtered – and store into a bottle.

MELON VODKA

Melons come in many varieties including yellow, water and – my personal favourite – the cantaloupe. Usually in Europe we use the soft flesh of a melon as a fruit. However, in parts of Asia it's a savoury snack when sprinkled with salt. Some are even preserved and pickled.

This melon infusion can be served over ice with a splash of pineapple juice and a twist of lemon or lime, in a glass rimmed with salt.

Ingredients
- 250ml vodka
- 1 slice of melon of your choice
- Sugar syrup, to taste (optional)

Method
1. After removing and discarding the rind, chop the melon slice into chunks.
2. Put the melon in the bottom of your container and cover with vodka.
3. Give the container a shake and leave in a dark place for 3–4 days. Give it a stir or shake every day.
4. Filter well through a cheesecloth-lined sieve or filter paper, and add sugar syrup to taste. Even though melons are usually sweet they're stuffed with water and the resultant infusion can seem thin and slightly tasteless without added sugar, which takes the infusion to a new height.
5. Bottle. If you're a patient person then a few days or even longer of maturation can add to the flavour. However, impatient infusers will often be rewarded with a great drink.

PASSION FRUIT – NECTAR OF THE GODS

Can there be a sweeter fruit? Some people believe that when the ancients make reference to the nectar of the gods, it's to the passion fruit that they're referring.

The plant was discovered in South America by 16th century Spanish colonists, after which the growing of passion fruits soon spread around the world. Its deciduous vine thrives in warm, sub-tropical climates, and today it's an important commercial crop in countries far from South America such as Australia, Hawaii, South Africa and Israel. Originally it was named *flor de las cinco llagas* or 'flower of the five wounds', after its distinctive purple flower, the petals of which were thought to represent the wounds received by Christ when he was crucified.

In Brazil, where the plants are thought to have originated, a refreshing drink made from the pulp of the fruits is sold on the streets.

Ingredients
- 250ml vodka
- 2–3 passion fruit
- Sugar syrup, to taste (optional)

Method
1. Halve each fruit, scrape out the pulp, including the seeds, and place them in your container. Discard the skins.
2. Cover with vodka, shake well and leave for 2 or 3 days.
3. Strain well, extracting as much juice as is possible, and add sugar syrup to taste. You might find it sweet enough as it is. Bottle. Serve on ice, with a slosh of tonic, a sprig of mint and some fresh passion fruit seeds.

PINEAPPLE INFUSION – A WELCOME GIFT

Pineapples were probably a favourite of the indigenous people who lived in South America in the countries we now call Brazil and Paraguay, but were first discovered by Europeans in 1493 on the Caribbean Island now known as Guadeloupe. The fruits were much prized when Christopher Columbus and other early discoverers brought pineapples back to Europe.

Sadly, attempts to cultivate the fruits in Europe failed, tropical conditions being required for them to grow. However, by the end of the 16th century Portuguese and Spanish explorers had introduced pineapples into many of their Asian, African and South Pacific colonies – countries in which pineapples are still grown today. More than 20 million pineapples a year are also grown in Queensland, Australia, where Lutheran missionaries introduced the plant in the 1830s. When visiting friends people often gave them as a welcome gift, a sweet alternative to a bunch of flowers.

Today pineapples are a true superfruit that we enjoy on pizza and burgers, in desserts and cakes, wrapped in prosciutto and as a canapé. And, of course, they're an essential component of the classic pineapple and coconut cocktail, the Pina Colada.

Ingredients
- 250ml white rum
- 1 section of fresh pineapple
- Sprig of fresh mint
- Sugar syrup, to taste (optional)

Method
1 Cut off and discard the pineapple skin.
2 Cut the pineapple into thin slices and put into a container. Cover with white rum and add the sprig of mint. Leave in a dark place for 7–10 days, remembering to shake occasionally.
3 Strain and bottle, adding a little sugar syrup if needed. The discarded pineapple pulp can be used for a boozy fruit salad. Serve on ice with a twist of lime.

POMEGRANATE VODKA

Native to the Middle East, the pomegranate can be traced through historical documents as far back as 4000 BC, and – appropriately for a fruit with so many seeds – it's regarded as a symbol of fertility in many cultures.

The red fruit grows from pretty red flowers and is between a lemon and a grapefruit in size. The white flesh inside the thick skin is full of several hundred edible seeds, or arils, and is consumed raw. A modern-day superfood, its juice is sweetened and thickened to make grenadine syrup for cocktails. Pomegranate plants are also often grown as bonsai trees.

Ingredients
- 250ml vodka
- Seeds from ½ a pomegranate
- Sugar syrup, to taste (optional)

Method
1 Scoop out the arils from the half pomegranate, taking care to leave the pith behind.
2 Place the arils into the container and give them a muddling. Cover with vodka and shake well. Leave for seven days.
3 Add sugar syrup to suit your taste. Strain well and bottle. Serve as shots on ice, or as a long cold drink with soda water or lemonade.

RASPBERRY VODKA

There can be few better things than raspberries picked from your garden or allotment. Though those from a pick-your-own farm are just as good. Traditionally the raspberry was a summer fruit in temperate climates. However, new cultivars have been developed that extend the fruiting season. They can come in a variety of colour, from yellow to purple, but red is the most common. Once infused the fruit creates a fabulously rich and tart liqueur that can be drunk neat or used for summer cocktails. Gin can be used in place of vodka.

Ingredients
■ 500g raspberries
■ 200g white sugar
■ 750ml vodka
■ Sugar syrup, to taste (optional)

Method

1 Wash the raspberries and throw out any bruised or bad fruit. Gently mash the fruit to start to release the juices and place, with the sugar, into a Kilner jar or other container. Pour half the vodka in to the jar, seal the lid, then turn upside down and give the jar a shake to mix the fruit and sugar together.
2 Remove the lid and add the remaining vodka and stir. Store in a cool dark place for 2–3 weeks, turning and shaking the jar every few days.
3 Strain the contents of the jar and filter again if it is a little cloudy. If the drink is not sweet enough add sugar syrup, a little at a time, until it reaches the taste you want.

4 Store in a bottle. Serve neat, or chilled in martini glasses rimmed with pink sugar with a splash of tonic water, fresh raspberries and a sprig of mint.

SAMPHIRE – INFUSION WITH A SALTY KISS

Samphire really does have the taste of the sea, which is unsurprising since in the UK it grows wild in coastal wetland and mudflats. Today it is a smart, fashionable ingredient, widely loved by celebrity chefs and sold in many fish shops.

There are two types – rock and marsh samphire – but it's the marsh variety that graces the plates in fashionable restaurants.

Sometimes called seaside asparagus, samphire is related to the beet family and is often still known as glasswort, from the former use of its ashes in the production of soda glass. The season for its small succulent green shoots is relatively short, but if found the plant makes an interesting infusion.

Ingredients
■ 250ml or so vodka or gin
■ 20 or so shoots of samphire

Method

1 Wash the samphire and pat dry with kitchen paper. Put the samphire into your container and give it a light muddling to start releasing the flavours.
2 Cover with your spirit of choice and leave for a couple of days.
3 Strain and bottle. If you're really impatient just give it a very good shake and leave to infuse for an hour or so.
4 To enjoy at its best, serve with a splash of dry vermouth over ice.

(Cath Harries)

SKITTLES – TASTES OF THE RAINBOW

Drinking alcohol is meant to be fun, and what could be more fun than the bright, garish colours of infusions made using Skittles? And it's so easy. The hard part is separating the sweets into their different colours. There are five colours in a pack, so anyone feeling that they want a colourful night of vodka shots can easily make five different colour infusions.

Ingredients
- 12–15 skittles, of the same colour
- 250ml vodka or white rum

Method
1 Put 12–15 Skittles of the same colour into your container, top up with your chosen spirit and the job's nearly done.
2 Seal the container and give a good shake. The Skittles will dissolve very quickly.
3 Let the infusion stand in a fridge overnight to allow the Skittles to completely dissolve. Strain, chill and you're ready to go. Serve in tiny shot glasses. If you prefer your drinks long and colourful then mix with lemonade.

STRAWBERRY GIN

Ideal as a summer drink, strawberry gin, like raspberry vodka and sloe gin is also much enjoyed at Christmas time.

Ingredients
- 750ml gin
- 500g strawberries
- Sugar syrup, to taste (optional)

Method
1 Wash and dry the strawberries, then cut into largish chunks. This helps releases the juice. Place into a large Kilner jar. Top up with gin and put into a cool dark place for 1–2 weeks. Shake the jar each day.
2 After 2 weeks, taste, if it tastes good it's ready, but don't be afraid to be patient and give it more time. Once you are happy with the flavour, strain the contents of the jar and filter through a cheesecloth-lined sieve or filter paper if it is a little cloudy.
3 If the drink is not sweet enough, add sugar syrup until it reaches the taste you want. Store in a bottle and serve neat, or on ice with soda water.

STRAWBERRY AND CHILLI VODKA

Fancy some summer heat? This liqueur should add some colour and temperature to even the coldest, darkest day.

The first iterations of this drink proved to be so fiery that they were almost undrinkable. However, the chilli boffins at the Dartmoor Chilli Farm, to whom we owe our thanks for this recipe, stuck to their guns and kept researching to perfect it.

Making this drink is easy. It only takes a few minutes. However, it's recommended that for the best flavour you should leave it for at least three months before consuming. If you don't like vodka, this recipe works equally well with gin. In addition raspberries or peaches can be used instead of strawberries.

Ingredients
- 500g strawberries
- 250g sugar
- 600ml vodka
- 5 tsp dried chilli flakes
- Sugar syrup, to taste (optional)

Method
1 Wash the strawberries then place in a pan together with the sugar and chillies. Heat gently, stirring occasionally until the juice from the fruits begins to run and the sugar is dissolved.

2 Transfer the mixture to a glass bowl and add the vodka. Give this a stir, then cover with cling film and allow to cool.
3 Every day for four days, remove the cover and stir the mixture.
4 On the fifth day, strain the mixture into a bottle. Seal and store for two months in a dark cupboard.
5 Taste, adding a little sugar syrup if necessary.

SWEET CHESTNUT BRANDY

Brazier-roasted chestnuts have to be one of the most glorious, warm, sweet tastes of a British winter. Today chestnuts aren't just for roasting over an open fire – they're also the main flavouring in many a nutty infusion, including this intriguing liqueur. Peeling chestnuts isn't easy, the best method is to boil them in plenty of water for 20 minutes, then leave them in the hot water while you peel them one at a time, wearing rubber gloves. Using a sharp knife, cut away the top of the skin, then peel away the rest to release the nut.

Ingredients
- 250ml brandy
- 500g peeled and roughly chopped chestnuts
- Sugar syrup, to taste (optional)

Method
1 Place the peeled nuts in a large Kilner jar and cover with brandy.
2 Leave for a couple of weeks. Taste and add a little sugar syrup if you think it's needed.
3 Strain and bottle.

TEA VODKA

Tea is often thought of as being a quintessentially British drink, well, we have been drinking it for more than 350 years, the first reference to tea in this country being in an advertisement in a London newspaper, the *Mercurius Politicus*, dating to September 1658. According to this a 'China Drink, called by the Chinese, Tcha, by other Nations Tay alias Tee' was being sold in a fashionable coffee shop. The drink caught on so much that, what do the British do in any crisis? Drink a cup of tea.

But the story of tea is much older. According to legend it begins in 2737 BC, when one day the Chinese emperor Shen Nung was sitting beneath a tree while his servant boiled some

water, and leaves from the tree blew into the boiling water. The Emperor, who was reputedly a renowned herbalist, decided to drink the serendipitous infusion that the wind had created. The tree was a *Camellia sinensis*, and the resulting drink was what we now call tea.

The array of leaf infusions that are available for infusing is almost bewildering, and many of them make interesting partners to a spirit. Green tea in particular is a good partner to vodka. But these are spirited infusions that are strictly for adults only. A vodka-infused tea makes an interesting contribution to a cocktail, poured over slices of lemon with ice and lemonade.

Ingredients
- 250ml vodka
- 1 teabag or 1 tbsp of loose tea leaves
- Lemon zest (optional)
- Sugar syrup, or honey, to taste (optional)

Method
1 Put the teabag or loose leaves in your container, plus lemon zest (if it's being used).
2 Add the vodka and leave for three or four hours.
3 Strain, taste and add some sugar syrup or a mixture of honey and hot water if you prefer it sweeter. If you're happy with it as it is, bottle.

TURKISH DELIGHT VODKA

Turkish delight has a long, sweet history, and is one of the oldest forms of confectionery in the world.

Before the 18th century honey and grapes were among the ingredients people could use to sweeten things, until the widespread availability of sugar from cane changed sweetening forever. In Turkey it saw the creation of the Turkish delight, which was said to have been created in the kitchens

of the Ottoman court. To produce it confectioners blended a concoction of sugar syrup, various flavourings, nuts and dried fruits then bound them together with mastic (gum arabic). The result is sublime.

Today the sweet is still a Turkish favourite, used to complement the bitterness of a Turkish coffee and sweeten the breath at the end of an evening meal. The artist Picasso is supposed to have munched on Turkish delight in order to help his concentration while painting.

Ingredients
- 250ml vodka
- 3–4 chunks of Turkish delight (about 35g)
- A dash of rose water (optional)

Method
1 You might like to rinse the chopped cubes of Turkish delight to remove the dusting of sugar.
2 Put the Turkish delight into your container and cover with vodka. Add a dash of rose water if you wish.
3 Shake and leave for at least ten days.
4 If you're happy with the taste, filter and bottle.
5 Serve neat in a martini or shot glass. You can also pour a little over an adult serving of homemade vanilla ice cream.

WERTHER'S ORIGINAL

Anyone who's ever seen the television advertisements for Werther's Originals, first broadcast in 1997, could be forgiven for thinking that it's an old English sweet brand. In it an elderly man offers one of the sweets to his grandson, and so a family tradition is handed down through the generations. Another advertisement saw the grandfather and grandson bonding together on a train journey, accompanied by a song that ended: 'When one who loves you says to you: You're someone very special too.' The advertisements were the very quintessence of Englishness. However, the same advertisement in the US had the actors with American accents and in Germany they spoke in German.

In fact the brand was launched in 1969, not 1869, and as the sweet's parent company is named after the village in Germany where they're made its name should actually be pronounced *Verters*.

The butterscotch-flavoured candy, made from sugar and dairy ingredients with a dash of salt, makes an interesting liqueur. And it's so simple.

Ingredients
- 250ml vodka
- 5–6 Werther's Originals, or other brand of butterscotch toffee

(Cath Harries)

Method

1 Unwrap the sweets, rewrap them in cling film and give them a bit of a bashing with a rolling pin.

2 Place the smashed sweets in your container and cover with the vodka.

3 Shake and leave for three or four days or until the sweets have dissolved, remembering to agitate them each day.

4 To make instant liqueur, put both ingredients into a container that has a good seal, place it in a dishwasher and put the machine on its highest heat. Run the container through one cycle and the sweets should have melted. Once cooled and chilled the liqueur will be ready to drink.

WHISKY GALORE – WELL, ALMOST

Can I make my own whisky? Well, probably not – home distilling isn't legal in the UK. And then there's the small matter of needing to mature it in an oak barrel for at least three years if you want to call your drink whisky.

However, it is possible to mimic at home some of the characteristics found in a whisky. The base, raw spirit from which whisky is made isn't a million miles away from vodka. All the colour in a whisky and most of the taste comes from the barrel in which it's matured. For a bit of fun, you can get bags of oak chips from a wine shop and see what flavour and colour they add to your spirit. The oak chips come in a variety of toastings and sources, American and French. American oak chips give a fruity character to the spirit. The French chips have a spicier touch. Medium-toasted chips can add almond and caramel flavours. Heavily-toasted chips produce more nutty and roasted flavours and will probably give the spirit a darkish brown hue. There are even chips which have been infused with sherry. There are many whiskies that are stored in oak barrels that once contained bourbon or sherry.

The amount of contact time you leave the spirit on the chips is up to you. It could be a matter of days or even months. However, the longer you leave it the greater the effect on the spirit will be. It's so easy to do.

Ingredients
- 500ml vodka
- Oak chips from a home wine-makers' shop
- Sugar syrup, to taste (optional)

Method

1 Use about half a teaspoon of oak chips for each 500ml of vodka, depending on how oaky you want the end result, and whether you have light or dark toasted chips. Some packets of oak chips recommend you wet them with boiling water beforehand.

2 Add the chips to the container, add the vodka and give a good shake. It's worthwhile shaking the container on a regular basis to ensure that as much wood as possible is exposed to the spirit.

3 Once you're happy with the infusion, which should have darkened and taken on some of the flavours from the wood, strain, add sugar syrup to taste, and bottle.

CHAPTER 8
INFUSED COCKTAILS

Making your own cocktails

Shake, rattle and roll or even muddle – liqueurs can be drunk before or after dinner in a traditional liqueur glass or late in the evening as a goodnight drink. But they don't have to be drunk just as a short or a shot – mixed with fruit juices or sodas they can also be enjoyed as a refreshing drink or one of the components of a cocktail?

Good cocktails have three main elements – the base spirit, a mixer and flavourings. Add to this some theatre and you're almost there. The base spirit gives the cocktail its main flavour and character; the mixer takes the base up to another level; and the flavouring gives the drink its sublime individuality.

Cocktails are all about balance – strong versus weak and sweet versus sour. The alcohol provides the strength, and the 'weak' aspect could be the flavouring in your liqueur or infusion. The sour can come from citrus fruits and the sweet is the sugar, which you may have already added if you've made a liqueur. The trick is knowing the flavours of your ingredients and how they work with other additions. You've been adjusting the sweetness of your liqueurs when you add sugar syrup, and the more you do this the better understanding of taste you'll have. Your own infusion or liqueur is likely to be the building block of the cocktails you make.

When creating cocktails, it's important to have a 'taste picture' in your head and remember that it's all about balance. Remember too that minimalism can be good, a drop of bitters or simply a twist of lemon or lime rubbed around the edge of the glass and then dropped into the drink can transform it to a new level.

EQUIPMENT NEEDED

Cocktail shakers, strainers, muddlers, bar spoons, knives, jiggers – there's a seemingly endless array of tools aimed at helping you make better cocktails. But suitable substitutes for what you need can be found in most homes. For instance, if you don't have a shaker, use a jam jar.

- **Jiggers** – a jigger is used to measure out the ingredients for a cocktail. Perfect cocktails, not just good ones, are all about exact measurements. A jigger is perfect if you don't know how to pour.
- **Bar spoons** – good for stirring and for pouring ingredients over the back of as they go into the cocktail. They can also be used to measure out small quantities of ingredients.
- **Strainers** – strainers allow cocktails to be poured while keeping the ice out. A fine strainer ensures that little bits of fruit flesh are removed. For most people a tea strainer is fine.
- **Citrus press** – the fresher your fruit juice the better your cocktail will be. A good press allows you to get the maximum goodness from your fruit.
- **Muddler** – essentially a tool, usually made of wood, that's used to crush fruit, herbs or spices to release essential flavour compounds needed for the drink.
- **Knife** – a small, sharp knife makes cutting fruit so much easier.

SOME TECHNICAL THINGS

■ **Shaking** – shaking mixes and cools down ingredients. It's important not to overfill the shaker. Half-full is fine. And don't overdo it – theatre is one thing, but you needn't shake for more than ten seconds.

■ **Stirring** – It's entirely up to you. Usually, shaken and stirred drinks are strained into their serving glass. As a general rule shake any drink that contains juice, dairy or eggs. These will look better in a glass and have better texture when they're a little foamy. Stir any drink that's made from just spirits.

■ **Blending** – making alcoholic slush puppies isn't for everyone, but whizzing up the spirit with ice in a blender can be useful.

■ **Muddling** – gentle muddling is preferable to energetic bashing. You're looking to release the flavours of the ingredients, not destroy them.

■ **Layering** – the heaviest part of the drink is poured in first. Subsequent layers can be added by pouring over the back of a spoon into the glass.

■ **Ice** – if you want to be really posh, use filtered or bottled water. The taste of tap water can be dominated by chlorinated flavours.

■ **Chilled glasses** – if you have space put glasses into a freezer before use. If the glass has a stem, try and hold it using this.

■ **Flavouring the rim** – dipping the rim of the glass into salt or sugar transforms some cocktails. But remember that less is more, don't overwhelm the drink with the salt or sugar.

■ **Fruit** – fresh and clean should be the order of the day.

■ **Glassware** – presentation is everything with a cocktail. The right glass or container can make a good cocktail great.

■ **Citrus** – to balance sweet tones add something sour. Those most used are lemons or limes. Freshly squeezed is usually best.

■ **Sweetness** – if you're using a liqueur you've made you already have some, from sugar syrup to the more complex cinnamon and orange peel-infused vanilla syrup. Even nettle syrup can add class to a cocktail.

■ **Spices and bitterness** – beginners should stick to simplicity, but bitters can add a kick to a cocktail. Bitters such as angostura, Peychaud's and orange bitters can be bought in the shops.

COCKTAIL RECIPES USING HOME INFUSIONS

Once you have tested and perfected your own home infusions, and are perhaps creating them in larger quantities, it is time to start using them in cocktails. Here are some suggested recipes to start you on your way to becoming an expert mixologist.

Sloe gin and tonic

For many people a well-made gin and tonic is the perfect pick me up. But to transform this classic drink into a herbal zinger, use sloe gin.

Serves 1

Ingredients
- 50ml sloe gin
- 120ml tonic water
- Fresh lemon or lime, to garnish

Method
1. Pour 50ml sloe gin into a tall glass half filled with cubed ice.
2. Top with the tonic water and serve garnished with a lime wedge.

Sloe and rum duet

Sloe gin also makes a perfect partner to a light rum. The addition of fresh lemon juice and mint makes a great fruity addition to the gin-soused sloes.

Serves 1

Ingredients
- 10 freshly picked mint leaves
- 50ml white rum
- 35ml sloe gin
- 35ml freshly squeezed lemon juice

Method
1 Fill the cocktail shaker with ice, remember don't overfill. Add the mint leaves, the white rum, sloe gin, and lemon juice. Give it a good shake.
2 Pour the mixture through your strainer into a long glass. Garnish with a mint leaf or two and serve.

Sloe gin with eggy fizz

Egg whites are used in many cocktails. They add body, and a rich sophisticated mouthfeel. Don't worry, they will not add the taste of egg, but they will make the cocktail feel silkily better. Use a very fresh, free range egg.

Serves 2

Ingredients
- 1 egg white
- 15ml fresh lemon or lime juice
- 50ml sloe gin
- 75ml soda
- Slices of lemon and lime, to serve

Method
1 Place the egg white, lemon or lime juice and sloe gin in a shaker. Give it a very good shake.
2 Add some ice to the shaker and give it a second good shake. Strain the liquid into two tall glasses and top with the soda.
3 Serve, garnished with slices of lemon and lime.

Merry cherries

Cherry brandy is one of the richest and most satisfying of sipping infusions. The sweetness of the cherries makes the perfect foil to the robust richness of the brandy.

Serves 1

Ingredients
- 50ml cherry brandy
- 25ml fresh lemon juice
- 1 dash bitters
- 120ml tonic water
- Slice of lime or lemon.

Method
1 Half fill the shaker with ice. Pour in the cherry brandy and lemon juice and add a dash of bitters. Shake well.
2 Strain the mixture into a glass. Top with the tonic water and garnish with a slice of lime or lemon.

Creamy, cherried brandy and rum

Adding cream to a cocktail brings a smooth silkiness to this sublime combination of brandy and rum.

Serves 1

Ingredients
- 50ml white rum
- 25ml cherry brandy
- 25ml single cream
- Cherry to garnish

Method
1 Half fill the cocktail shaker with ice, add the rum, cherry brandy and cream.
2 Shake well and strain into a glass.

Double cherry brandy

Brandy might seem to be an old fashioned drink, but it is undergoing a renaissance. Today, it is as likely to be drunk by the Hackney hipster as their grandma in Gateshead.

Serves 1

Ingredients
- 30ml cherry brandy
- 30ml brandy
- 20ml lemon juice
- Zest of lemon

Method
1. Add ice and all the ingredients to the shaker. Give it a good shake.
2. Strain into a glass and serve.

Elderflower Martini

For many the elder is just a shrub which grows alongside roads. Yet, both its flowers and small dark red fruits were highly valued by our forebears to add flavour to many drinks and foods.

Serves 1

Ingredients
- 50ml elderflower-infused vodka
- 10ml chamomile tea, strained and chilled
- 10ml dry vermouth
- Lime slices, to garnish

Method
1. Put ice into the shaker, add the elderflower vodka, chamomile tea and vermouth. Shake well.
2. Strain into a glass and serve with a slice of lime.

Cranberry vodka with a touch of fizz

Cranberry based cocktails are often considered as a refreshing drink for a hot summers day. But, don't despair if it's a cold winter's day, they can be as warming as they are refreshing.

Serves two

Ingredients
■ 75ml Cranberry flavoured vodka
■ 75ml cranberry juice.
■ A dash of sugar syrup
■ Sparkling white wine

Method
1 Add ice to the shaker. Pour in the vodka, cranberry juice and a dash of sugar syrup.
2 Shake well and strain into glasses. Top up with the sparkling white wine.

Blackberry and apple pie

Serves 2

Ingredients
■ 100ml blackberry vodka
■ 50ml apple juice
■ 6 fresh blackberries
■ Double cream

Method
1 Put the blackberries into the shaker and muddle. Add the blackberry vodka, apple juice and some ice. Shake well.
2 Pour the mixture through a strainer into chilled martini glasses. Carefully, float double cream over the top by pouring over the back of a spoon.

Zesty vodka orange with a tequila twist

Serves 2

Ingredients
- 25ml orange infusion (vodka or brandy)
- 25ml gold tequila
- 50ml fresh lime juice
- A dash of angostura bitters
- 25gm salt
- Orange slices, to garnish

Method
1 Rub the rim of the glasses with the lime juice. Dip into the salt.
2 Add ice to the shaker and pour in the orange infusion, tequila and remaining lime juice. Shake well.
3 Strain the ingredients into the glasses and garnish with orange slices.

Getting hot with a chilli bloody Mary

Can there be a better drink for a lazy morning at home, when someone suggests brunch – a bloody Mary. Long and satisfying, it is often best to upscale the ingredients and make it by the jug.

Serves 2

Ingredients
- 2 dashes Worcestershire sauce
- 100ml chilli vodka- for a salty hit use a vodka infused with bacon
- 500ml tomato juice
- 30ml lemon juice
- Celery salt, to taste
- Cayenne pepper, to taste
- Tabasco sauce (optional)
- 25g salt
- Stick of celery, or red chillies, to garnish

Method
1 Put the ice into a shaker. Dash the Worcestershire over the ice and pour in the chilli vodka, tomato juice and lemon juice. Shake vigorously.
2 Spread the salt on a small plate. Rub the rib of the glasses with lemon juice, then dip into the salt. Half fill the glasses with ice.
3 Strain the bloody Mary into the glasses. Depending how spicy you like it you can add a pinch of celery salt, a pinch of cayenne pepper and a dash of Tabasco.
4 Stir the drink. Garnish each glass with a chilli or a piece of celery. Leave the Tabasco on the side so more can be added to suit your taste.

FORAGED COCKTAILS

Perhaps the most rewarding type of infused spirits are the ones made from foraged ingredients. When you then use those to make your own cocktails, there is even greater satisfaction. For the cocktails that follow as many of the ingredients as possible were found in the wild, including perhaps the most sought after foraged ingredient – black Périgord truffles, which brings a mysterious, earthy note to a wheat and barley-based vodka. The truffle season starts in December and lasts through only until January, meaning that a whole year's supply must be purchased in one go, before being frozen to make the vodka throughout the year.

These cocktails were created by Johan Svensson, Black Moth's cocktail connoisseur. Where possible he used foraged ingredients to make them. Each of them makes 1 generous serving, or 2 more moderate servings.

Black Moth Juniper Vodka & Tonic

Serves 1
Foraged ingredients: bay leaves, juniper.

Ingredients

For the juniper syrup
- 1 cup caster sugar
- 1 cup water
- 4 juniper berries, slightly crushed
- 2 bay leaves

For the vodka and tonic cocktail
- 50ml Black Moth Truffle Vodka
- 15ml juniper syrup
- 10ml fresh lemon juice
- small pinch of salt
- Tonic water
- Grapefruit twist, to serve

Method

1 To make a supply of the juniper syrup combine the sugar, water, juniper berries and bay leaves in a small saucepan. On a gentle heat, stir until the sugar is completely dissolved, then increase the heat and bring to a boil.
2 When the mixture boils, reduce the heat and simmer until slightly thickened, about five minutes. Remove from heat and allow to steep for 15–20 minutes.
3 Strain the syrup, discarding the berries and bay leaves, and transfer to a container with a tight-fitting lid. Cover and refrigerate until ready to use. This and other flavoured sugar syrups can be used in many different cocktails or infusions,
4 To make the vodka & tonic cocktail, mix chilled vodka, syrup, lemon juice and salt over lots of cubed ice in a hi-ball glass, stir gently to mix.
5 Top with a quality tonic water such as Fever Tree, stir again, and serve garnished with a pink grapefruit twist.

Elderflower Martini

Serves 1
Foraged ingredients: elderflowers, chamomile.

Ingredients

- handful fresh elderflowers, washed
- 50ml elderflower-infused vodka
- 10ml chamomile tea, strained and chilled
- 10ml dry vermouth

Method

1 Pat dry the washed elderlfowers with kitchen paper. Decant the vodka into a sterilised glass bottle or jar and add the elderflowers. Leave for 24 hours then fine-strain through muslin cloth.
2 To make the martini, pour the vodka, chamomile tea and vermouth over lots of cubed ice in a mixing glass and stir.
3 Strain the cocktail into a chilled tasting glass and serve.

Queen of the Sea Martini

Serves 1
Foraged ingredients: sea lettuce.

Ingredients
For the sea lettuce and pepper water
- 200g sea lettuce (washed and rinsed)
- 10 black peppercorns
- 1 litre water

For the queen of the sea martini
- 60ml vodka
- 10ml sea lettuce and peppercorn water
- 5ml Caol Ila 12-year-old Islay whisky

Method
1. To make the sea lettuce and pepper water, slice the sea lettuce into julienne strips, add the water and peppercorns and bring to the boil.
2. Gently simmer for 30 minutes, then leave to cool. Only a small amount is needed for the cocktail but the remaining liquid makes an ideal stock for using in stews and soups. It can be stored in a freezer.
3. To make the cocktail, gently stir all ingredients over cubed ice in a mixing glass then strain into a chilled vintage martini glass.

Sea lettuce (*Ulva lactuca*) is a bright green leafy highly nutritious seaweed, found on most rocky sea shores in the zone between the high and low tide mark. The leaves may appear flat, thin, broad, and often rounded or oval and look a little like lettuce leaves.

To harvest sea lettuce, cut the leaves with a knife, leaving the root-like fixing to the rock. As with all foraging, never take too much from one place, or more than you will need. Once you get the leaves home, wash thoroughly to remove all traces of sand.

Truffle Nettle Julep

Serves 1
Foraged ingredients: nettles.

Ingredients
For the nettle syrup
- 1kg young nettles, freshly picked
- 500ml water
- 750g caster sugar

For the truffle nettle julep
- 50ml Black Moth Truffle Vodka
- 15ml nettle syrup
- 15ml fresh lime juice
- Two drops truffle bitters

Method
1. To make the nettle syrup, strip the nettle leaves from the stalks, discard these and wash the leaves. Pat dry with kitchen paper. Quickly blanch a handful of the smallest, youngest nettles for 30 seconds in boiling water and finely chop. Set aside.
2. Bring 500ml water to the boil slowly and pour in 750g caster sugar. Heat, stirring, until all the sugar is dissolved.
3. Add the remaining picked nettles to the hot syrup with two strips of lemon zest. Remove from the heat and leave to cool.
4. Strain the liquid and stir in the chopped nettles. Chill until ready to use.

5. To mix the julep, stir half the vodka, 15ml nettle syrup, the lime juice and bitters in the bottom of a julep tin and add a scoop of crushed ice.
6. Churn the ingredients through the ice.
7. Add the remaining 25ml vodka and churn again. Pour into a serving glass, top with crushed ice and garnish with a nettle (or mint) sprig.

Coastal Mary

Serves 1
Foraged ingredients: sea salt, sea beet, homegrown tomato.

Ingredients
For the tomato mix
- 150g fresh tomatoes, washed
- 250g sea beet, washed and blanched briefly in boiling water
- Tabasco and Worcestershire sauces, to taste

For the coastal Mary
- 50ml vodka
- 120ml tomato mix
- 15ml fresh lemon juice

Method
1. To make the bloody Mary tomato mix, roast the tomatoes in an oven until soft.
2. Blend the tomatoes with 250g blanched sea beet in a food processor, add a dash of Tabasco, a dash of Worcestershire sauce, plenty of black pepper and enough water to make a thick sauce. The consistency should be like a smoothie. Cool and chill. Any unused sauce can be stored in the refrigerator.
3. To make a Coastal Mary, pour the Black Moth Truffle Vodka into a large wine glass filled with cubed ice. Add 15ml lemon juice and 120ml bloody Mary tomato mix and stir until completely blended.
4. Serve garnished with lemon and a crab claw.

Sea beet grows on land close to the sea shore. It has glossy green oval leaves and is a close relative of beetroot, chard and spinach. The leaves are best picked in springtime.

Blackberry Bellini

Serves 1

Foraged ingredients: blackberries.

Ingredients

For the blackberry purée
- 250g blackberries, washed
- 50g caster sugar
- 100ml water
- Zest of orange

For the blackberry bellini
- 25ml vodka
- 25ml blackberry purée
- Prosecco or champagne

Method

1 To make the blackberry purée put the blackberries and sugar into a small pan with 100ml water. Bring to the boil, then simmer for 5 minutes until the fruit is soft. Remove and allow to cool. Add the zest of orange.

3 Tip the contents of the pan into a blender or food processor, and whizz to a purée. Strain through a sieve, rubbing it through with the back of a spoon. It will keep in a refrigerator for up to 2 weeks.
2 To make a blackberry bellini, shake vodka and blackberry purée with cubed ice and double-strain into a chilled champagne flute. Top up with prosecco/champagne.

Strawberry punch

Serves 1

Ingredients

For the strawberry purée
- 250g strawberries, washed and stalks removed
- 50g caster sugar
- 100ml water
- Zest of orange

For the strawberry punch
- 35ml Black Moth Truffle Vodka
- 25ml strawberry purée
- 10ml fresh lime juice
- 80ml ginger ale

Method

1 To make the strawberry purée, put the washed strawberries and sugar into a small pan with 100ml water. Bring to the boil, then simmer for 5 minutes until the fruit is soft. Remove from the heat and allow to cool. Add the Orange zest.
2 Tip the contents of the pan into a blender or food processor, and whizz to a purée, then strain through a sieve, rubbing it through with the back of a ladle or spoon. It will keep in refrigerator for up to 2 weeks.
3 To make the punch, add Black Moth Truffle Vodka, lime and strawberry purée into a shaker filled with cubed ice.
4 Shake hard and strain over ginger ale and cubed ice. Gently stir and serve garnished with a strawberry and basil sprig.

CHAPTER 9
COOKING WITH INFUSIONS

Spirited recipes

Infusions and liqueurs aren't just great in a glass, they can also add something special to many food dishes. There are no hard and fast rules, so don't be afraid to experiment. Liqueurs and infusions can add a wow factor to many sauces and marinades and many will also work brilliantly with fruit and ice cream.

BRANDY LIQUEUR MARINADE

This all-purpose marinade can add a touch of glamour to many dishes. It can be used with beef, chicken, pork and even fish.
Makes approx 300ml

Ingredients

- 250ml soy sauce
- 1 tbsp brown sugar
- 1 tsp minced ginger
- 1–2 garlic cloves, peeled and minced
- 1 tbsp brandy liqueur
- 1 tbsp sesame oil
- Salt

Method

1 Combine all the ingredients in a large jar and shake to mix. Refrigerate for 24 hours before using it to marinade your meat or fish.
2 To use, pour over your main ingredient, ensuring it's covered all over, and marinate for 1–2 hours in the refrigerator before cooking.
3 Cook the marinated meat or fish in a frying pan with a little oil, or on a barbecue.

SLOE-ROASTED LAMB

Serves 6–8

Ingredients

- 2kg leg of lamb
- 100ml sloe gin
- 2 sliced cloves of garlic
- 2 large onions, peeled and quartered
- 2 leeks
- tbsp olive oil
- Salt and pepper

Method

1 Preheat the oven to 200°C/180°C fan/Gas 6.
2 Place the quartered onions and leeks in a roasting dish. Put the lamb on top of the vegetables. Make incisions in the lamb and push in slices of garlic.
3 Mix the sloe gin with the oil and drizzle over the lamb. Cook in the oven for 1½ hours, basting occasionally.
4 Remove the meat from the oven and allow to rest for 20–30 minutes while you make the gravy from the juices in the pan and prepare the vegetables. Slice the meat and serve with the gravy.

PHEASANT BREAST WITH APPLES AND BRANDY

Serves 6

Ingredients
- 6 pheasant breasts
- 100g butter
- 900g eating apples, peeled, cored and sliced
- 400ml double cream
- 3 tbsp apple brandy liqueur
- Salt and black pepper

Method
1 Season the pheasant breasts with salt and pepper.
2 On a medium to high heat, melt half the butter in a frying pan. Fry the breasts until golden brown. Once browned on both sides, transfer them to a plate.
3 In the same pan, melt the rest of the butter, add the sliced apples and fry for three or four minutes. Remove from the pan and set aside.
4 On a medium to high heat, deglaze the pan with the apple brandy. Then stir in the double cream and turn the heat down to a simmer. Return the breasts, plus any meat juice that have been released, to the pan. Allow the sauce to reduce for 3–4 minutes, then add the apple slices to the pan and heat through for another minute.
5 Serve immediately with vegetables of your choice.

ORANGE BRANDY CHOCOLATE TRUFFLES

Makes approx 15–20 truffles

Ingredients
- 50ml orange brandy
- 250g dark chocolate, chopped into bits
- 280ml double cream
- 50g butter

Method
1 Pour the cream into a saucepan, add the butter and heat until almost simmering. Turn the heat down low and add the chocolate pieces. Stir until the mixture has melded together.
2 Take off the heat. Stir in the orange or cherry brandy and pour the mixture into a bowl.
3 Once cooled put the bowl into a fridge.
4 Once hardened, scoop out balls with a melon baller or spoon dipped in warm water. Put the balls on to greaseproof paper. Alternatively, lightly coat your hands with sunflower oil and roll the truffles between your palms.
5 For extra flavour you can roll the balls in cocoa powder flavoured with orange zest or crushed pistachio nuts.
6 Store in a fridge for two or three days, or freeze them for a month or so. Nicely packaged they make excellent gifts.

Liquid Christmas presents

One of the joys of making infusions and liqueurs is being able to give them away. And presents don't have to be just for Christmas – your generosity will be appreciated at any time of year. Drinkable gifts are perfect for people who seem to have everything or enjoy a particular style that's hard to match. They also give you a chance to show off your cherished creations.

Spirited liqueurs therefore make ideal presents, and are particularly useful if you want to make a personalised gift. There's always something very special about giving away an infusion you've made from fruit you've picked, such as sloes and damsons. It could be something exotic made from tropical fruit bought from a local supermarket, or an indulgent cream liqueur in a bauble sized little Christmas bottle.

And as you'll have seen by now, infusions are so easy to make. Cranberries, orange juice, orange zest, sugar and vodka are such simple ingredients, yet they'll make a drink that oozes originality and creativity. Put them together and within a few weeks you'll have something very special. If you know someone who likes a good bloody Mary, then consider a vodka infusion, perhaps made with chilli for a hot kick, or even bacon if they like a salty kiss.

The key thing is to make sure you put your gift into a nice bottle or container, which you can personalise with a handmade label. Charity shops are a good source of interesting bottles. Swing-top bottles or corked bottles always look especially interesting. However, do make sure the bottles are thoroughly cleaned before use. It would be even more sensible to sterilise them. Finally the addition of pretty ribbons and tags will turn your infusion into a nicely packaged gift that really does say 'I think a lot of you.'

LIQUID CHRISTMAS PUDDING

Ingredients
- 100g mixed dried fruit, currents and sultanas
- 1 cinnamon stick
- 1 tsp ground mixed spice
- 2 cloves
- ¼ whole nutmeg, finely grated
- finely grated zest of 1 orange
- finely grated zest of 1 lemon
- 350ml vodka
- Sugar syrup, to taste (optional)

Method
1 Other than the sugar syrup, mix all the ingredients together in a bowl or other container.
2 Pour the vodka over and cover.
3 Put in a cool place and leave for three days.
4 Place in the fridge and leave for another three or four days, stirring once each day.
5 Taste, and add sugar syrup if you think it's needed.
6 Filter thoroughly through a cheesecloth-lined sieve or filter paper. You might have to do this more than once.
7 Decant into a nice bottle.

BOOZY CHICKEN BREASTS
Serves 4

Ingredients
- 4 chicken breasts
- Seasoned flour, for coating
- Butter, for frying
- 2 hearty garlic cloves, peeled and finely chopped
- 600–750ml chicken stock
- 300ml double cream (single can be used if you prefer)
- 2 tbsp orange liqueur

Method
1 Coat the chicken in the seasoned flour and brown it on both sides in butter in a frying pan. Remove the chicken from the pan and set aside.
2 Add the garlic to pan and soften, but don't burn. Pour in the stock and heat until simmering. Place the chicken breasts in the pan and simmer for about 30 minutes.
3 When the sauce has reduced, remove the chicken and stir in the double cream and orange liqueur.
4 Bring to the boil to thicken slightly, then serve the chicken with the sauce poured over the top.

CLASSY PANCAKES WITH AN ALCOHOLIC TWIST

Crêpe suzette is a classic French dessert. According to food myth it was created by accident, when the liqueur being used caught fire!

Makes approx 12 pancakes

Pancake ingredients
- 150g plain flour
- pinch of salt
- 200ml milk
- 10ml water
- 2 eggs
- 25g butter, melted
- sunflower oil, for frying

Orange sauce ingredients
- 3 tbsp caster sugar
- 250ml freshly squeezed orange juice
- Finely grated zest of 1 orange
- 1 tbsp orange brandy liqueur
- 50g unsalted butter, melted.

Method
1 To make the pancake batter, sift the flour and pinch of salt into a bowl and make a well in the middle. Mix the milk and water together.
2 Break the eggs into the well and start to whisk, slowly at first.
3 While doing this, pour in the milk and water mixture. Keep whisking until the batter has come together. Whisk in the melted butter.
4 Lightly oil a frying pan, and put on medium heat.
5 Spoon or ladle just enough batter to thinly cover the base of the pan, swirling it until bottom is evenly coated. The thinner the coating the lighter and more delicate your pancake will be.
6 Cook on one side for about 50 seconds, until it's golden. Carefully flip it over and cook it on the other side for 30 seconds.
7 Carefully, using a spatula or by sliding, take the pancake out of the pan and place on a plate. Keep making pancakes until the mixture is used. Stack the pancakes interleaved with pieces of baking paper.
8 To make the sauce, put the sugar into a non-stick frying pan and heat over a low heat until it begins to melt and turns a dark colour.
9 Take off the heat and carefully pour in the orange juice and liqueur. Put the pan back on a low heat, add the butter, bring to the boil and simmer until the hot caramel looks glossy. Turn off the heat and add the orange zest.
10 Put the pancakes into the pan. Fold into quarters if necessary.
11 Serve immediately, with a garnish of zest and toppings of your choice – cream, ice cream or some fresh berries.

BOOZY ETON MESS
Serves 4

Eton mess is a classic dessert that's very easy to make, especially if you use shop-bought meringues. Yours can be named after a school of your choice. Make this just before serving, it won't stand for too long before the meringues get soggy.

Ingredients
- 200ml double cream
- 6 meringue nests, broken into irregular pieces
- 400g fresh strawberries, washed and quartered
- 50ml strawberry liqueur

Method
1 Whip the cream in a large bowl until soft peaks form.
Stir in the broken meringues.
2 In another bowl mix the strawberries with the liqueur.
3 Take a large serving bowl or individual wine glasses and add a layer of the cream and meringue followed by the strawberry mixture followed by a further layer of the meringue mix. Top with a garnish of strawberries.

RHUBARB FOOL – ADULTS ONLY

Serves 2

So what do you with rhubarb when you're made your infusion? Well, only a fool would throw the pulp away.

Ingredients
- 300g rhubarb, strained from a liqueur
- Sugar to taste
- 300ml double cream
- Small bunch of mint, leaves only

Method
1 Put into a pan the pulp left over after straining and bottling your rhubarb infusion.
2 Gently warm through, allowing some of the juice to evaporate.
3 Add a tablespoon or two of granulated sugar to suit your taste. Add more sugar if you have a sweet tooth. Allow to cool completely.
4 Whip the cream until it has nice soft peaks.
5 Fold in the cooled rhubarb and chill in the fridge for a good hour.
6 Serve in bowls with a garnish of mint leaves.

CHOCOLATE LIQUEURS

Likewise, what do you do with sloes, damsons, cherries or other soft fruit once your infusion has been strained off? They might not look much, but they'll still have some alcohol in them and probably lots of flavour too.

Ingredients
- Leftover damson or raspberry pulp, or similar fruit
- Bar of dark or white chocolate

Method
1 First remove the stones from the fruit, if there are any.
2 Take the bar of chocolate and carefully melt in a saucepan on a very low heat.
3 Mix in the fruit and pour into a small shallow dish or individual ice cube trays. Allow to cool and then put in fridge to set.

FORTIFIED PORT-STYLE DRINK

Boozy fruit left over from making a sloe or gin infusion can be used to make another infusion. Instead of a clear spirit, though, douse the fruit in a stronger flavoured spirit, be it rum, brandy or whisky.

Ingredients
- Leftover pulp
- 100g sugar
- 750ml bottle red wine
- 100–200ml rum, brandy or whisky

Method
1 Add 100g of sugar to the fruit and cover with wine.
2 Put in a container, which should be filled right to the top and sealed. It's important the container is filled to the top to avoid oxidation.
3 Leave for at least eight weeks.
4 Alternatively, cover the used fruit with some still cider, the stronger the better. Then put in a container and seal and leave for several weeks.

FRUITY AND BOOZY SAUCE

Method
1 Take used fruit from an infusion and ensure all the stones are removed.
2 Blitz in a blender and pour over ice cream. Alternatively, chop the fruit and use it in any cake, biscuit or pudding instead of dried fruit.

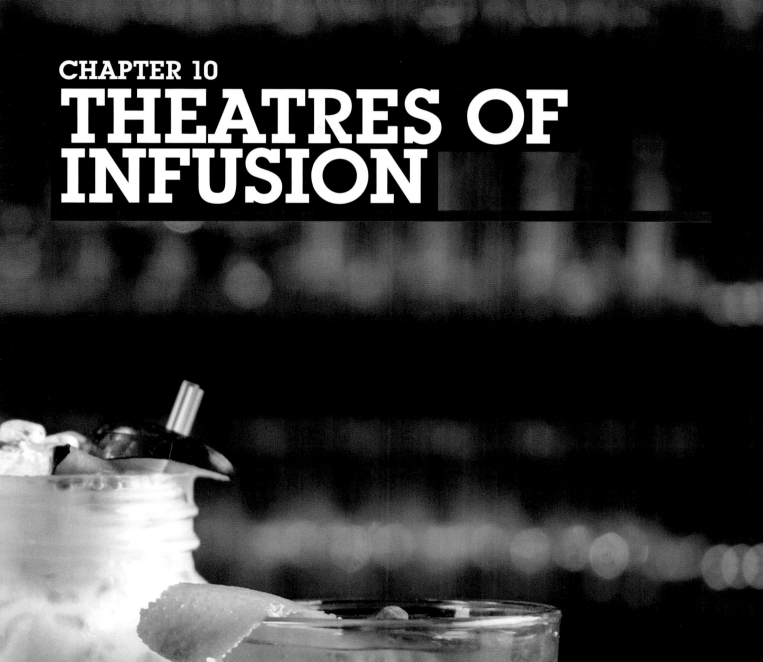

Where better to go to see liqueurs and infusions being used to make classy, classic cocktails than one of the world's best bars – three of which are in London.

Lobby Bar

One Aldwych, WC2B 4RH
www.onealdwych.com
Nearest tube: Covent Garden
Signature drink: seasonal cocktails

▲ **Outside One Aldwych the London traffic roars, inside there is an air of serenity and relaxation.** (Courtesy One Aldwych)

A certain kind of hotel lobby bar never fails to impress. It is coolness personified. So if you want to impress someone, then the bar at the fashionable One Aldwych hotel has to be the place to go. It's a place where the staff understand the starring role that great infusions and liqueurs play in sublime cocktails.

The Lobby Bar is one of the capital's most uber-cool places to sip cocktails, which is why it was recently named one of the top five hotel bars in the world. Its theatre of cocktail making is managed by Lobby Bar manager Pedro Paulo, who has worked there since 2011.

The large, graceful space is filled with intriguing modern sculptures and huge displays of fresh flowers on Perspex plinths rising up towards the tall ceilings, and large graceful

▼ **The smart, graceful Lobby Bar is the stage for a theatre of expert and delicious infusions.** (Courtesy One Aldwych)

windows flood the area with light, which dapples on the polished limestone floor. The ethos is smart and laid back, and the cocktails are class in a glass. It's a great place for a drink before going off to see something at one of the many nearby theatres and for people walking along the Strand who fancy some serious relaxation.

The cocktail list is extensive and varies with the season, and despite the five-star status of the hotel and the ingredients that go into the drinks the prices are reasonable. Its drinks include cocktails inspired by Hendrick's Gin and its unique mix of botanicals. One special is a summer infusion that's dramatically served in a chilled porthole. The gin is mixed with a dash of white port and rose lemonade that's infused with fresh apple, ginger and lemon balm.

▲ **The bar boasts a menu of seasonal cocktails using the freshest ingredients.** (Courtesy One Aldwych)

Anyone wanting a caffeine fix should try the Espresso Martini, in which vanilla-infused vodka, coffee liqueur, hazelnut liqueur and a shot of espresso are brought together in a drink that nears perfection.

Food offerings include sharing platters. Oysters are also available when in season.

MODERN TAKE ON AN OLD FASHIONED

Pedro Paulo loves to create new interpretations of old classics. One of his favourites is his riff on an Old Fashioned using Woodford Reserve bourbon. This classic drink has its roots deep within the history of cocktails, having been developed in New York in the early 19th century.

Like all great drinks, the components seem so simple – Woodford Reserve, a hotel-made Old Fashioned syrup, spirit-macerated cherries and a dash of angostura bitters. The drink is then served, chilled over a hand-carved piece of ice that's been cut from a 25kg crystal-clear block.

The cherry infusion is made in the hotel to a carefully guarded recipe. Bourbon, spices, cloves, vanilla and lemon are infused and then some grappa is added. The infusion macerates in large glass jars for at least two months before some sugar syrup is added. 'All the ingredients make sense and they're meant to enhance the bourbon,' says Pedro. 'But it's the cherry liqueur which is the star of the show.' To add to the drama, the drink is made in front of the customer.

Ingredients
- 30ml double shot bourbon
- 15ml hotel-infused cherry liqueur
- 2 dashes of angostura bitters
- Strip of orange peel
- Cherry from the infusion

Lobby Bar Old Fashioned Cocktail
Preparation and performance are essential to the creation of a great cocktail.

1 A mixing glass is chilled with a large piece of ice, which is then removed. (Photographs Cath Harries)

2 One by one the ingredients are added to the mixing glass.

3 Once mixed, the drink should be poured through a strainer into a serving glass with ice.

4 As a final flourish, the glass is decorated with an infused cherry and strip of orange.

Shochu Lounge

37 Charlotte Street, W1T 1RR
www.shochulounge.com
Nearest tube: Goodge Street
Signature drink: Plum Plum

An underground bar that specialises in Japanese-inspired cocktails and spirits.

There's something dark and mysterious about this cool underground bar, located under Roka, a stylish Japanese restaurant. The bar takes its name from the Japanese distilled drink shochu, which is similar to vodka and originated from the Kagoshima district of Kyushu Island.

Shochu comes in two forms: otsu rui, which is made from rice, sweet potatoes, rye, corn or raw sugar; and ko-rui, a purer distillation made from molasses. The drink is aged in *kumes* or barrels and then infused with a diverse variety of fruits, herbs and spices, ranging from pine needles and raspberries to plums and catnip. The otsu rui is best drunk straight, with a dash of water or some ice, rather like a malt whisky. The koi rui has little in the way of aroma and is often used as a base for cocktails. Shochu is often mixed with hot or cold tea or a fruit juice such as grapefruit, peach or orange.

The trendy bar, with its low tables and chairs, sells a range of shochu cocktails and really feels like a little bit of Japan in London. The bar's signature drink is Plum Plum, a mix of shochu flavoured with plums and plum vodka. According to legend the drink is good for people's health. It has inspired a number of cocktails said to be imbued with health-giving

▲ **The Shochu Lounge, in a basement underneath Goodge Street, London, is a little bit of Japan.** (Courtesy Shochu Lounge)

qualities. The ki lazubeli shu is supposed to improve memory, and jasmine flower shu is good for coughs, sneezes and probably several other disorders.

Shochu is renowned for serving good spicy food, its menu being the same as the excellent Roka restaurant upstairs. The bar's staff are happy to talk customers through the long menu of oriental delicacies.

Making your own green tea shochu infusion

Ingredients
- 100g sencha green tea
- 500ml shochu

Method
1. Take a clean 500ml Kilner jar or similar.
2. Add the sencha green tea, then pour on the shochu. Leave to infuse for one month.
3. Strain and bottle, and it's time to enjoy your green tea infusion.

Try it on the rocks or with a splash of hot water. It's also a great base for green tea cocktails. But don't be constrained by the recipe – try any variety of green tea. All should work well. And the people at the Japan Centre in London say it's not just green tea that's fun to infuse. Traditional Japanese fruits like yuzu citrus or spices like togarashi chilli pepper also produce interesting drinks. Some Japanese chefs recommend steeping konbu kelp or bonito flakes to create savoury shochu infusions for use in dishes like miso soup or teriyaki chicken.

Those who can't wait for a month can make a quick sencha cocktail by making the sencha with a bottled mineral water and tea, using cold infusion. Mix two teaspoons of tea with 500ml of bottled mineral water, leave it in a fridge for 30 minutes and shake.

Baltic Bar

74 Blackfriars Road, SE1 8HA
www.balticrestaurant.co.uk
Nearest tube: Blackfriars
Signature drinks: selection of infused vodkas and vodka cocktails

This multi award-winning bar and restaurant deserves all the plaudits that have been heaped upon it.

Vodka is the first choice of drink for many customers at this great bar, but those who think it is a spirit best drunk with a dash of coke or a splash of lime cordial are in a for a surprise here. If they visit the Baltic's Amber bar, situated on the corner of The Cut and Blackfriars and a short walk from South Bank and the Tate Modern, they enter a world that's a cool, classy homage to vodka drinking.

The grain-based spirit is the centre of most things, though there's a good range of other spirits, wines and beers. But icy fresh and very, very cool vodka is the spirit for most people who enjoy drinking here. It's the most versatile and chic spirit, whether drunk on its own or performing either as a bit player or the star in a world-class cocktail. Classic vodka is clear as melted snow, but the range on sale at the Baltic reflects the array of flavoured vodkas available from Eastern Europe, with colours ranging from pale yellow for lemon vodka to black for liquorice.

Created by Jan Woroniecki, the Baltic's Amber bar is sleek and as classy in design as an Apple iPad. It's relaxing and buzzy and a great way for people to unwind at the end of a working day. It operates semi-independently from the restaurant and has an extensive range of blinis, soup, potato pancakes and charcuterie. However, it's the vodkas, many with naturally infused flavours, that star.

Mixologist Charles Vexenat has created some new classics including Mon Cherrie Cooler. Its ingredients include house-infused cherry wódka shaken with fresh passion fruit and Mozart black chocolate liqueur and lengthened with pressed apple juice. If that's not to your liking then try a Rabarbara – Potocki wódka stirred with Martini rosato, rhubarb liqueur and Peychaud bitters.

The skill of the staff isn't just in their knowledge of the repertoire of ingredients they have available, but also in their ability to match them and create something that should suit most people's tastes.

▲ The Baltic Bar not only makes its own infusions, it also boasts a huge range of branded spirits, especially vodka. (Cath Harries)

◤ Large jars of infusions are more than just decorations at the Baltic, they play a leading role in many cocktails. (Cath Harries)

▶ The bar has its own small still, which is often in use, and stands behind the bar. (Cath Harries)

GLOSSARY

Absinthe – A once illegal anise-based aperitif drink with an infusion of wormwood, considered by some to be hallucinogenic and dangerous.

ABV – Alcohol by volume is the alcohol strength of a drink measured as a percentage in relation to the liquid as a whole. 40% ABV is equal to 40% alcohol and 60% water.

Advocaat – A Dutch liqueur made with egg yolks, sugar and brandy.

Agave – Mexican plant that's used to make tequila and mescal.

Alembic – Alternative term for a pot still. They're still used for making cognac.

Allspice – A ground spice made from an unripe berry with an aroma reminiscent of a cinnamon, cloves and nutmeg.

Amaretto – An Italian liqueur with a sweet almond flavour.

Angostura bitters – The most popular bitters, made in Trinidad and produced with a secret blend of aromatic spices.

Anisette – A liquorice-tasting liqueur made from anise seeds.

Aperitif – A drink taken before a meal to stimulate the appetite.

Aperol – An Italian bitter aperitif flavoured with oranges.

Apricot brandy – Apricot-flavoured brandy.

Aquavit – A spirit from Scandinavia flavoured with herbs and spices.

Armagnac – A region of France famed for making a brandy of the same name.

Aroma – The smell or perfume of a drink. Some people call it a bouquet.

Bar spoon – Long-handled spoon used for stirring and measuring ingredients. Many have a disc on top that acts as a muddler.

Bar strainer – A strainer that fits over the top of a cocktail shaker and prevents ice, fruit and other ingredients from being poured into a serving glass.

Benedictine – A herb-flavoured liqueur produced by the Benedictine monks of France.

Bitters – Herb and root extracts or liqueurs flavoured with herb and root extracts, traditionally thought to help stimulate the appetite and aid digestion.

Black raspberry liqueur – A black raspberry-flavoured liqueur (see Chambord).

Blue Curaçao – Blue-coloured Dutch West Indian curaçao orange liqueur. Produced in Holland.

Boston shaker – Cocktail shaker consisting of a glass and metal beaker that fit together to make a sealed container.

Bourbon – Classic US style of whisky, which by law must be made from a mash of not less than 51% corn grain. The spirit is matured in new, white oak barrels that have previously been charred or thermally degraded.

Brandy – A spirit distilled from a grape wine.

Cachaça – A Brazilian spirit made from fermented sugar cane.

Calvados – A spirit distilled from apples, usually from Normandy.

Campari – An Italian bitter wine with a distinctive red colour.

Carbon dioxide – Carbon dioxide (CO2) is created during fermentation as yeast converts sugar into alcohol.

Cassis – Dark red blackcurrant liqueur.

Chambord – A black raspberry-flavoured liqueur produced in Burgundy.

Chartreuse – Yellow and green herbal liqueurs produced since 1605 by the Carthusian monks of La Grande, from a secret recipe consisting of over 100 alpine herbs.

Chill filtration – Spirits are often chilled before bottling to remove natural substances that can cause them to become cloudy if stored at low temperature or diluted with water.

Clearic – New make spirit, straight from the still. Clear in colour and high in strength, it was a popular drink with distillery workers.

Coffey still – Patented in 1830 by former Irish Inspector-General of Excise Aeneas Coffey, this type of still revolutionised distilling. Also known as the column, continuous or patent still, it allowed large quantities of spirit to be distilled continuously and much more quickly than in traditional pot stills. Originally it comprised two tall columns, the first being the analyser that separated the spirit from the wash, while the second, known as the rectifier, further concentrated the spirit.

Cognac – Region of France famed for making a distilled wine (brandy) of the same name.

Cointreau – A bitter-sweet French citrus liqueur made with Seville oranges and lemons. Produced by the Cointreau family since 1849.

Congeners – Chemical constituents of the distilling process.

Continuous distillation – Using a long column or Coffey still, the wash is passed over steam under high pressure. It produces higher strength alcohol than a pot still.

Cooper – Someone who makes a wooden barrel. Once the craft of coopering was widespread, but today it's principally kept alive only by the spirits industry.

Crème – A thick and concentrated infusion of fruit in neutral grain spirits. Commonly made from blackcurrants or raspberries, but can be from any fruit or nut source.

Crème de banana – Banana-flavoured liqueur.

Crème de cacao – A cocoa liqueur flavoured with roasted cocoa beans and vanilla.

Crème de cassis – A French liqueur made from blackcurrants.

Crème de framboise – A French liqueur made from raspberries.

Crème de menthe – A creamy peppermint-flavoured liqueur. Can be red, green or white.

Crème de violette – Violet-flavoured liqueur.

Curaçao – Orange-flavoured liqueur produced mainly in France and the Netherlands, but originating from the Caribbean. Made from the bitter peel of oranges grown on the island of Curaçao in the West Indies. It comes in many colours, but is most commonly blue.

Decanting – Separating the infusion from its ingredients.

Digestif – A drink taken after a meal to settle the stomach and aid digestion.

Distillation – The act of boiling a base alcohol to release the alcohol as a vapour, which is then collected as it cools (condenses), becoming a far stronger alcoholic liquid. It's the basis of all sprits, infusions and liqueurs.

Drambuie – Scottish whisky and honey liqueur, first made on the island of Skye, Scotland, in 1745. Now produced in Edinburgh.

Dry vermouth – French-made, herb-flavoured wine used in making drinks such as the Martini and Manhattan.

Dubonnet – A French brand of aperitif wine made from aromatics.

Eau de vie – The 'water of life', French term for a spirit distilled from a fruit wine.

Everclear – A US brand of grain alcohol available at concentrations of 95% alcohol (190 proof) and 75.5% (151 proof).

Fermentation – The process of turning fermentable sugar into alcohol. Yeast cells feed off the sugar, converting it into carbon dioxide and a water product we call alcohol.

Fernet-Branca – A bitter, aromatic spirit made from over 40 herbs and spices.

Float – An ingredient carefully poured so that it floats on top of a drink.

Fortification – The addition of a spirit, usually brandy, to a wine to increase its strength and character.

Frangelico – An Italian liqueur made from hazelnuts.

Frappe – A very cold liqueur.

Galliano – Gold-coloured Italian liqueur flavoured with herbs.

Genever – Juniper-flavoured spirit from Holland, an early variant of gin.

Gin – A clear spirit flavoured with juniper berries.

Grand Marnier – An orange liqueur.

Grappa – Clear Italian brandy distilled from the remains of grapes used in wine production.

Grenadine – A sweet pomegranate syrup used to add colour and flavour to drinks.

Jägermeister – A German herbal liqueur.

Jigger – A cocktail maker's tool used to measure ingredients accurately. Also called a shot.

Julet – Originally a sweet syrup, now a family of spirit-based cocktails, flavoured and decorated with fresh mint.

Kahlúa – A coffee-flavoured liqueur made in Mexico.

Kirsch – A brandy distilled from fermented cherry juice.

Kirshwasser – Clear cherry-flavoured eau-de-vie, mainly from France and Switzerland.

Kumme – Colourless Dutch liqueur flavoured with caraway.

Pastis – A French anise-flavoured liqueur served as an aperitif.

Lillet – French herb-flavoured liqueur based on wine and Armagnac.

Limoncello – A distinctive liqueur made with the skin of fresh lemons from Southern Italy.

Liqueur – A strong alcoholic drink made from distilled spirits with additional flavouring added, such as herbs and spices.

London dry – A style of gin, probably the best-known. It should be fresh, clean and light.

Maceration – The process of steeping fruits, herbs and other ingredients in alcohol to extract flavour.

Mandarin Napoleon – Belgian brandy-based liqueur flavoured with tangerines.

Maraschino – Italian cherry-flavoured liqueur, usually colourless but may be red.

Mashing – The conversion of starch into sugar by being steeped in warm water.

Melon liqueur – Spirit-based, melon-flavoured liqueur.

Mezcal – Spirit similar to tequila made from agave plants. Most is made in the Mexican state of Oaxaca, but it can be produced elsewhere. The worm found in the bottom of the bottle in some brands originated in the 1940s as a marketing ploy.

Midori – A green-coloured, melon-flavoured liqueur made in Japan.

Mirabelle – Plum eau-de-vie, or colourless brandy.

Molasses – Also called black treacle, molasses is a sugary syrup produced during the conversion of sugar cane or sugar beet into sugar.

Monte Alban – A mezcal named after an Aztec settlement in Oaxaca, Mexico, where it's been made since the 16th century.

Mouthfeel – The texture of a drink in the mouth.

Muddler – Cocktail tool used for bruising and crushing fruit and herb leaves.

New make – The clear alcoholic liquid that comes off a still.

Nocello Walnut – A walnut-flavoured liqueur from Italy.

Nose – The aroma of a drink. When it comes to taste the nose is far more powerful than the taste buds on our tongue. Time spent nosing or sniffing a liqueur opens up a new world of tastes and aromas.

Nosing glass – A tulip-shaped glass used to taste whisky. It has a narrow opening so that the liqueur can be swirled, allowing the aromas to rise and be concentrated in the nostrils.

Ouzo – An unsweetened anise-flavoured liqueur from Greece.

Pastis – Anise-based aperitif that turns cloudy with water, often known by the brand names Pernod, Ricard or Mon Pastis.

Patent still – Another name for the Coffey still.

Peter Heering – A world-renowned cherry-flavoured liqueur. Produced since 1818 in Copenhagen, Denmark.

Peychaud Bitters – Originally created in 1830 by Antoine Peychaud in Haiti. Now produced in New Orleans by the Sazerac Company.

Phylloxera – A blight that devastated Europe's vineyards in the 19th century, caused by tiny insects that kill vine roots. It was originally imported from the United States on American vine stock.

Pimms – Pimm's No 1 is a gin-based liquor made in England from dry gin, liqueur, fruit juices and spices.

Pisco – A Peruvian grape-based brandy, often used to make a Pisco Sour.

Pot still – A pot still is a huge copper kettle. The alcoholic spirit is driven off from the fermented liquid as a vapour and then condensed back to liquid.

Pousse-café – A drink poured in layers to float on top of each other, which gives its name to a narrow, straight-sided stemmed glass.

Prisonnière – Term used when an apple or pear is grown inside a bottle that's then filled with either Calvados or Poire William.

Proof – Measurement of the strength of spirits, expressed in degrees, calculated using a hydrometer. Although still employed in the USA, the proof system has now been superseded in Europe by a measurement of alcohol strength as a percentage of alcohol by volume (ABV). 80 proof equals 40% ABV.

Racking – The process of siphoning wine from one container to another. It's typically used to describe the process of filling bottles.

Rum – A spirit distilled from an alcohol made from sugar cane. Light, medium and heavy-bodied flavour variations exist as do variations in colour when not clear. Often flavoured with spices or fruit flavours.

Rye whiskey – Mainly American and Canadian whiskey, which must be made from a mash containing at least 51% rye.

Sambuca – An Italian liqueur flavoured with anise and elderberries, sometimes served with flaming coffee beans.

Schnapps – A distillation from grain or potatoes that's often flavoured with aniseed or caraway. In Scandinavia it's called aquavit.

Scotch – Whisky made in Scotland.

Slivovitz – A Croatian version of plum brandy.

Sloe gin – A British favourite, a liqueur made by steeping sloe berries in gin. Previously homemade but now available commercially.

Soju – A clear Korean grain alcohol.

Sour – A spirit-based cocktail containing sugar and lemon or lime juice.

Southern Comfort – a whiskey liqueur from New Orleans with an orange-peach flavour.

Steeping – Soaking a material in water or alcohol to extract the flavour.

Strega – Italian herb-flavoured liqueur made with over 50 botanicals and coloured with saffron.

Sugar syrup – A sweetener for infusions and cocktails, made by dissolving sugar in boiling water.

Sweet vermouth – An Italian-made, herb-flavoured wine. Used in making drinks such as Rob Roys and Manhattans.

Tennessee – Tennessee whiskey is made in the eponymous US state and is characterised by a charcoal filtration process (known as the Lincoln process) that's said to produce a purer, smoother drink.

Tequila – A spirit distilled from the sap of the agave plant.

Tia Maria – Popular Jamaican rum-based coffee liqueur.

Tincture – An alcoholic extract of plant or animal material or spices, achieved by percolation.

Triple distillation – The practice of distilling whisky three times rather than the usual twice. It's a traditional characteristic of Irish whiskey and Lowland Scottish whisky making.

Triple sec – Colourless, orange-flavoured liqueur.

Twist – Small slice or wedge of citrus squeezed over a cocktail to flavour it

Vermouth – Wine-based aperitif flavoured with extracts of wormwood. Both sweet and dry vermouths are widely used in cocktails.

Vodka – A neutral spirit that can be distilled from any plant rich in starch or sugar, including grain, molasses and potatoes.

Wash – The name used in a whisky distillery for the mixture of alcohol, particles and congeners generated during the fermentation process.

Whiskey – Irish whisky. Also the name used for whisky in the USA.

Wort – The sweet liquid produced by mashing.

Yeast – The living microorganism that's vital for the fermentation process. Without it there'd be no alcoholic drinks. It feeds on the sugary wort and produces alcohol and carbon dioxide as by-products.